THE VEGETARIAN BABY FOOD COOKBOOK

FOR 6-12 MONTH OLD BABIES

Dr. Jyoti Kumari Srivastava
Dr. Mandala Sathwik

BlueRoseONE.com
Stories Matter
NewDelhi • London

BLUEROSE PUBLISHERS
India | U.K.

For permissions requests or inquiries regarding this publication,
please contact:

BLUEROSE PUBLISHERS
www.BlueRoseONE.com
info@bluerosepublishers.com
+91 8882 898 898
+4407342408967

ISBN: 978-93-7310-217-7

Typesetting: Manisha Rawat

First Edition: April 2026

Disclaimer

Please note that the recipes in this cookbook are intended as supplementary ideas to enhance your baby's diet with variety and natural flavours. We strongly advise against completely shifting your baby's feeding schedule based solely on these suggestions. Instead, continue incorporating your traditional, regional, or cultural food preferences as the foundation of their meals, using our recipes as add-ons to introduce new tastes and textures. Always observe your baby closely for any signs of non-suitability, such as allergies, digestive issues, or discomfort. If any such reactions occur, stop using the recipe immediately and consult your nearest medical care facility. The authors and publishers assume no responsibility for any errors, untoward reactions, or consequences arising from improper feeding practices. Be watchful, prioritize your child's well-being, and enjoy the rewarding experiences of parenting.

To Our Beloved, Jaiwik

Your radiant soul inspired the creation of

The Vegetarian Baby Food Cookbook

For 6- to 12-Month-Old Babies

Your boundless curiosity and joyful spirit motivated every recipe, filling our hearts with a sense of purpose.

May you continue to brighten our world.

With all our love,

Your Parents

From our Hearts

In a world where expectant parents face a whirlwind of challenges—external stressors from bustling homes and demanding workplaces, internal shifts like hormonal changes, and the realities of today's nuclear families—the journey to parenthood calls for resilience, intention, and a deep commitment to nurturing health. In this era of abundance, where convenience often tempts us toward packaged foods for our little ones, it's easy to overlook the profound impact of wholesome, natural nourishment. Yet, as doctors of Naturopathy, we've always been guided by the wisdom of naturopathy, aligning our lives with Nature's rhythms to maintain vitality. Even with this foundation, our own path to parenthood revealed its complexities. Our child arrived not through natural, a reality that brought both blessings and challenges. One of the most emotional was the delay in natural milk production, leaving us with a question that pierced our hearts: How can we provide our baby with the nourishment needed to build a strong foundation for lifelong immunity and health?

This question, born from our own experience, awakened us to a shared truth: countless new parents may face similar gaps in providing optimal nutrition during those critical early months, especially when balancing busy schedules or relying on nannies and nursemaids to assist with feeding. As time unfolded, we nurtured our child with a blend of mother's milk and formula, always carrying the quiet ache of those initial days when natural feeding felt just out of reach. Yet, this challenge became our inspiration. Blessed to raise our child in environments with clean air and vibrant, wholesome agricultural produce, we began to listen closely to our baby's cues. Those subtle hints guided us to introduce vegetarian foods thoughtfully, sparking a journey of discovery that transformed our approach to nourishment—helping us track our baby's preferences and ensure every meal prepared by us aligned with our values.

To our joy, the recipes we crafted—rooted in nature's bounty and tailored for our little one—unlocked remarkable milestones in our child's development. Each vibrant puree, each carefully blended meal, seemed to weave health, harmony, and happiness into our baby's growth. It was a revelation that inspired us to create *The Vegetarian Baby Food Cookbook*.

This book is our heartfelt offering to you—new parents seeking to nourish your 6- to 12-month-old with intention and love, while navigating the temptations of processed options and empowering you to monitor your baby's choices and what trusted helpers like nannies might provide. We hope that these recipes, born from our journey and infused with care, will empower you to cultivate your child's health and joy in those precious early months. May this cookbook be a trusted companion as you enter the beautiful, transformative adventure of parenthood.

With all our hearts,

The Authors

How to Read this Cookbook

Welcome to The Vegetarian Baby Food Cookbook, a guide crafted from our personal journey as naturopathic doctors and parents. This book is designed to support you through the exciting phase of introducing solid foods to your 6- to 12-month-old, emphasizing vegetarian recipes that align with the principles of Indian Naturopathy for optimal health and development. To make the most of it, we recommend approaching the content in a way that builds your knowledge progressively while allowing flexibility for your family's unique needs.

➢ **Start with the Heart: The Introduction and "From Our Hearts"**

Begin here to connect with the book's foundation. Our preface, "From Our Hearts," shares our own story of navigating parenthood's challenges, including delays in natural milk production and the transition to blended feeding. This sets the tone for why we've focused on intentional, vegetarian-based nourishment. Reading this first will inspire you and help you appreciate the philosophy behind the recipes—rooted in resilience, listening to your baby's cues, and using wholesome, vegetarian ingredients to stimulate lifelong immunity and joy.

➢ **Build Your Foundation: Chapters 1 and 2**

Dive into the essentials next. Chapter 1, "Understanding Your Baby's Nutritional Needs," explains the key nourishments for this age group, drawing from naturopathic principles to ensure balanced, plant-based diets. Follow with Chapter 2, "Getting Started with Baby Food Prep," which covers practical tools, safety tips, and techniques for preparing purees and blends at home. These chapters equip you with the knowledge to confidently begin your baby's food journey.

➢ **Progress by Age: Chapters 3 Through 5**

The core of the book is organized by your baby's developmental stage, making it easy to tailor recipes to their age and readiness:

- **Chapter 3:** First Foods (6-8 Months) - Focus on smooth, simple purees to introduce flavours gently. Start here if your baby is just beginning solids.
- **Chapter 4:** Textured Blends (8-10 Months) - Move to slightly chunkier options as your baby develops chewing skills.
- **Chapter 5:** Textured Meals and Finger Foods (10-12 Months) - Explore self-feeding ideas with more complex textures to encourage independence.

We suggest reading these sequentially as your baby grows, but feel free to reference earlier chapters for refreshers or mix recipes across stages based on milestones like teething or appetite changes.

➢ **Enhance Your Experience: Chapters 6 Through 8**

Use these as ongoing resources:

- **Chapter 6:** Special Considerations and Tips - Address common issues like allergies, portion sizes, or incorporating clean, seasonal produce into meals.
- **Chapter 7:** FAQs and Troubleshooting - Quick answers to questions that may arise, such as handling picky eating or adjusting for environmental factors.
- **Chapter 8:** Home-Made Porridge - Premixes and Coconut Milk - Bonus recipes for convenient staples that complement the main dishes.

Refer to these chapters whenever you need troubleshooting or inspiration, especially when adapting recipes to your lifestyle.

➢ **Tips for Navigation and Use**

- **As a Reference Tool:** While the book flows logically, treat it like a companion—jump to age-specific sections or the index for quick lookups.
- **Personalize It:** Listen to your baby's cues, just as we did, and experiment with the recipes. Note what works in the margins for future reference.

- **Revisit Often:** Parenthood evolves, so return to earlier sections as needed, and let the book's emphasis on harmony guide you toward a nurturing, stress-free experience.

We hope this structure empowers you to nourish your little one with love and confidence. Enjoy the adventure!

The Authors

Introduction: Welcoming Your Baby to the World of Flavours

As the baby's needs grow, it becomes essential to provide proper nutrition. When we talk about adequate nutrition, it does not only refer to artificial or packaged foods; instead, natural foods play a more significant role. This book emphasizes the importance of homemade, wholesome baby food recipes for babies aged 6 to 12 months. In today's fast-paced and non-biological lifestyle, a mother's health is also at risk, as she is the primary source of nutrition for the baby until at least 5-6 months.

Research indicates that babies who are exclusively breastfed for at least 5-6 months develop a stronger immune system and a more diverse gut microbiome, making them less susceptible to respiratory infections, gastrointestinal infections, and ear infections.[1] Now, we are faced with the question of why the 6-month mark is vital for introducing solid foods. The reasons include:

1. **Digestive Development**: The digestive enzymes of a baby, low at birth, start to mature at the age of 6-12 months, when the baby develops the enzymes required for digesting fats, carbohydrates, proteins, and other nutrients.
2. **Increased Nutritional Needs**: As babies grow, their nutritional demands increase, and breast milk or formula alone may not suffice to support their rapid development.

By now, we are clear about the baby's age and the introduction of solid foods. Now we try to clarify the understanding of homemade foods and packaged foods.

1 Branger, B., Bainier, A., Martin, L., Darviot, E., Forgeron, A., Sarthou, L., ... & Troussier, F. (2023). Breast-feeding and respiratory, ear and gastro-intestinal infections, in children, under the age of one year, admitted through the paediatric emergency departments of five hospitals. *Frontiers in Pediatrics*, *10*, 1053473.

Homemade vs. Packaged Foods

Packaged foods may list the nutrients on the label, but the key question is whether the baby's digestive and absorption systems can effectively take them in and process them. Also, packaged foods might contain preservatives or other chemicals that aren't fully broken down and could increase the baby's toxin exposure. In comparison, homemade baby food—made with fresh ingredients like lentils, rice, vegetables, and mild spices—provides pure, wholesome nutrition tailored to your baby's needs. Based on Indian culinary traditions, these recipes offer familiarity, affordability, and cultural connection.

This book empowers parents to embrace the joy of preparing homemade baby food, blending tradition with modern nutritional insights. From creamy dal purees to soft idli bites, you will be guided through creating meals that nourish your baby's body and introduce them to the vibrant flavours of India.

Contents

1: Understanding Your Baby's Nutritional Needs

1.1 Developmental Milestones and Nutrition for 6- to 12-Month-Olds

Between 6 and 12 months, your baby is transforming from a curious infant to an active explorer, achieving remarkable physical, cognitive, and social milestones. In Indian households, where food is a cherished part of family life, providing nutrient-rich, homemade meals tailored to these developmental stages ensures your baby's vitality. This chapter explores key developmental milestones and the nutritional requirements that support them, with Indian-inspired foods and scientific insights to guide you.

1.1.1 Physical Development

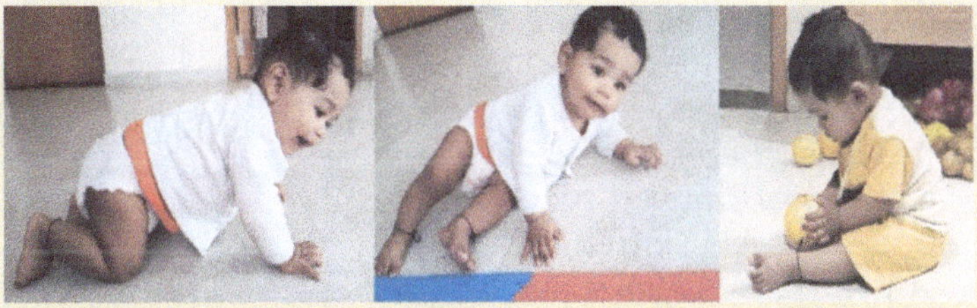

6–8 Months

- **Motor Skills**: Babies begin sitting with minimal support, rolling over both ways, and may start scooting or crawling. They develop a pincer grip (thumb and forefinger) for grasping objects.
- **Oral Skills**: The tongue-thrust reflex fades, enabling swallowing of pureed foods. Babies coordinate their mouths to accept food from a spoon and may attempt to hold it.

Tip: Introduce nuts and seeds individually for 3 days to check for allergies, as they are potential allergens. Start with a small amount (½ tsp powder) for 8+ months.

- **Nutritional Support**: Iron-rich foods like moong dal porridge or ragi porridge are vital, as iron supports muscle development and oxygen transport. Healthy fats (e.g., ghee) boost the brain's development and provide energy for the baby's movements.

9–12 Months

- **Motor Skills**: Babies may pull to stand, cruise along furniture, or take their first steps. Fine motor skills improve, allowing them to pick up small, soft foods and self-feed.
- **Oral Skills**: Chewing begins, even without teeth, as gums are strong enough for soft textures. Babies can handle mashed or minced foods and finger foods, strengthening jaw muscles.

Tip: Diced steamed vegetables (beetroot, carrot, sweet potato) support self-feeding and motor skill development.

- **Nutritional Support**: Protein (lentils) supports muscle growth, while calcium (e.g., ragi) strengthens bones for standing and walking. Varied textures like mini idlis or vegetable khichdi encourage chewing.
- **Scientific Insight**: Physical milestones depend on myelination of nerves (fat coating for nerve signals) and muscle growth, both supported by fats and proteins.[2] Iron deficiency can delay motor development by impairing oxygen delivery to muscles and the brain.[3]

---

2 astronot. (2025, May 25). *Myelination is Important Because: Child's Development - Scienceinsider.blog*. Scienceinsider.blog. https://scienceinsider.blog/myelination-child-development/

3 Theola, J., & Andriastuti, M. (2025). Neurodevelopmental impairments as long-term effects of iron deficiency in early childhood: a systematic review. *Balkan Medical Journal, 42*(2), 108.

1.1.2. Cognitive Development

6–8 Months

- Babies become more curious, recognizing familiar faces and objects. They explore cause-and-effect (e.g., banging a spoon) and show interest in their surroundings.
- **Nutritional Support**: Iron and omega-3 fatty acids (e.g., powdered flaxseed, introduced safely) are crucial for brain development. Vitamin A (e.g., carrots, spinach) supports vision for exploration.

Tip: Pureed spinach with rice provides iron and vitamins for cognitive growth.

9–12 Months

- Object permanence develops (knowing objects exist when out of sight), and babies may mimic actions or sounds. Problem-solving emerges, like reaching for food on a plate.
- **Nutritional Support**: Zinc (e.g., from lentils, ground pumpkin seeds) and B vitamins (e.g., from unpolished rice) support memory and neural connections. Diverse flavours from mild Indian spices (e.g., cumin) stimulate sensory development.

Tip: Vegetable khichdi with a pinch of turmeric offers zinc and sensory variety.

Scientific Insight: The brain grows rapidly, with synapses forming at a high rate. Iron and zinc deficiencies, if not addressed, can impair cognitive development.[4]

4 Black, M. M. (2003). Micronutrient deficiencies and cognitive functioning. The Journal of nutrition, 133(11), 3927S-3931S.

1.1.3. Social and Emotional Development

6–8 Months

- Babies bond closely with caregivers, showing excitement during feeding or play. They express preferences (e.g., reaching for a favourite food) and respond to emotions.
- **Nutritional Support**: Feeding at the family table fosters bonding. Breast milk or formula provides comfort, while new foods like papaya puree introduce variety.

Tip: Feeding varied purees during family meals strengthens emotional connections.

9–12 Months

- Babies show personality, expressing likes/dislikes (e.g., pushing away food) and mimicking family behaviors. They enjoy interactive feeding, like picking up soft mini idlis.
- **Nutritional Support**: Encouraging self-feeding with finger foods builds confidence. Vitamin D (from supplements) supports mood regulation and immunity.

Tip: Soft mini idlis/pancakes during family meals promote independence and social engagement.

Scientific Insight: Social interactions during feeding stimulate oxytocin release, strengthening bonds. Nutrient deficiencies can affect their mood.

1.2. Feeding Readiness

Requirements needed for successful starting of feeding include:

- **Ability to sit up**
- **Good head control**
- **Disappearance of the tongue thrust reflex**

- **Ability to grasp food in their palm**
- **Ability to turn their head away to signal they are full**
- **Showing an interest in food**

1.3. Feeding Tips for Parents

- **Start Slow**: Begin with 1–2 teaspoons of varied purees, increasing to 3 meals and 2–3 snacks by 12 months.
- **Start with Iron-Rich Foods**: Offer foods like mashed dal or ragi porridge first, as breast milk or formula alone may not provide enough iron after 6 months.
- **Balance with Breast Milk or Formula**: Continue breastfeeding or formula (with iron) as the main food source until 12 months, adding solids gradually (1 meal at 6 months, increasing to 3 meals and 2–3 snacks by 12 months).
- **Introduce Variety Safely**: Try one new food every 2-3 days to check for allergies. Stop if you notice rashes, vomiting, or breathing issues, and consult a doctor.

- **Patience with New Foods**: It may take 15–20 tries for your baby to accept new flavours like spinach or beetroot. Offer small amounts without forcing.
- **No Added Sugar or Salt**: Avoid adding sugar, jaggery, or salt, as these can harm developing kidneys and encourage unhealthy preferences.
- **Family Mealtime**: Include your baby at the family table, using a highchair or on a caregiver's lap, to mimic mealtime traditions and nurture social skills.
- **Texture Progression:**
    - 6 Months: Smooth purees
    - 7–8 Months: Mashed foods
    - 9–12 Months: Soft finger foods
- **Avoid Choking Hazards**: Skip whole nuts, grapes, or raw vegetables until age 4. Cut foods like bananas or parathas into small, safe pieces.
- **Supplements**: Check with your doctor about vitamin D supplements and other nutritional requirements.
- **Special Considerations**
    - ✓ **Premature Babies**: May need delayed introduction of solids; consult your paediatrician for fitted guidance.
    - ✓ **Vegetarian Diets**: Indian vegetarian diets are nutrient-rich but may lack iron or fat. Include ragi, lentils, and ghee, and consult your paediatrician for advice.
    - ✓ **Allergies**: Introduce potential allergens (e.g., ground nuts) one at a time after 6 months, as early exposure may reduce allergy risk.

1.4. Nutritional Needs for Your Growing Baby

After birth, the diet/nutrition of infants, especially for the first 2 years, is very important as most of the organs, including the brain, are still developing. However, it is important to understand that to gain an ideal weight and good health and nourishment during pregnancy, the nutritional state of the mother should be in good condition before pregnancy. It is known as pre-pregnancy nutrition. For example, Iron deficiency during pregnancy may decrease the birth weight of infants.[5] owever it si important to unsdHowever iProtein requirements vary with age; more proteins are required by growing infants and children.

Before 6 months of age, the perfect food for the human infant is that intended by Nature for its sustenance. Failing in the supply of mother's milk, substitutes may be used, and in some cases with very satisfactory success, but they are never so perfect or so much to be depended upon as the milk of a normal and healthy mother. Breastmilk alone meets all your baby's energy and nutrition needs.

Food groups for a balanced diet to meet the daily nutritional requirements of the baby (7 to 12 months)[6]

S.No	Food Group	Quantity in grams
1.	Cereals/ Millets	25
2.	Pulses & Beans	12
3.	Green Leafy Vegetables	20
4.	Vegetables	25
5.	Roots & Tubers	20
6.	Fruits	40 - 60
7.	Nuts	7
8.	Milk/Curd (ml)	Milk - roughly 580 ml per day
9.	Fats & Oils	10

1.5. Feeding and Nursing. – The nursing of a baby would seem to be the very simplest of all things, and yet there are common mistakes which are so detrimental to the welfare of the child that it is well to emphasize a few important rules in regard to infant feeding. Two of the most important mistakes are those of ***overfeeding*** and ***irregularity.*** Most babies are very much overfed, and there is no doubt that much of the prevalent illness among infants is due to this fact. Irregularity is also a cause of digestive disturbance and general functional derangement.

5 Georgieff, M. K. (2020). Iron deficiency in pregnancy. American journal of obstetrics and gynecology, 223(4), 516-524.

6 Table: from Dietary Guidelines for Indians, 2024 by ICMR-National Institute of Nutrition, Hyderabad

Regularity in feeding is a very important matter in infancy, allowing each meal to be digested before partaking of another, and establishing the habit of being hungry and having the hunger satisfied at the same hours each day. It is a common thing for mothers to fear that their baby is not getting enough nourishment, but in many more cases, they should fear the excess of feeding that is inclined to bring on disease. All books on the care of children have formulas or tables of the number of feedings for babies of different ages, but if anything, one should discount them somewhat to get the very best results. That is to say, one or two fewer feedings per day, at longer intervals than is suggested in the table for a particular age, will sometimes prove more satisfactory. But in all cases, the parents should map out a special timetable suited to their own baby, and adhere to this strictly in order that the regularity may not be interfered with.

The stomach of the newborn infant is small, being perpendicular and looking somewhat like a part of the intestines that has been dilated. At seven or eight months, intervals of three and a half hours should be allowed, with perhaps five daily feedings.

2: Getting Started with Baby Food Prep

Preparing homemade baby food is a rewarding way to ensure your child receives nutritious, wholesome meals fitted to their needs. This chapter outlines the essential tools, food safety practices, and ingredient selection tips with a focus on Indian households and scientific principles to ensure safety and nutrition.

2.1. Essential Kitchen Tools and Equipment for Making Baby Food

Equipping your kitchen with the right tools makes baby food preparation efficient, safe, and cost-effective. Here's a curated list of essentials:

- **Blender or Mixer Grinder**: A high-powered mixer grinder is ideal for creating smooth purees. For smaller batches, a compact blender or a hand blender works well. These ensure uniform texture, critical for infants (6–8 months) transitioning to solids, as smooth purees reduce choking risks and aid digestion.
- **Pressure Cooker with Steamer Basket**: A pressure cooker can be used with a steamer basket for steaming vegetables and fruits. Steaming retains more nutrients compared to boiling, which can cause significant nutrient loss.
- **Steel or BPA-Free Storage Containers**: Stainless steel air-tight containers are ideal for storing purees. Glass or steel containers are perfect for refrigeration. However, avoiding BPA-free storage containers is recommended as they can release microplastics even when they are not heated.
- **Fine Mesh Strainer**: A fine mesh strainer, commonly used for tea or spices, helps remove seeds, skins, or fibrous bits from purees, ensuring a smooth texture for younger babies.
- **Potato Masher or Fork**: For soft foods like bananas, boiled sweet potatoes, or chikoo (sapota), a simple masher or fork creates a rustic texture suitable for babies 9+ months, encouraging chewing skills.
- **Peeler and Chopping Board**: A sharp peeler and a wooden/steel/marble chopping board are essential for prepping vegetables/fruits. Choose a board dedicated to baby food to avoid cross-

contamination with spices.

- **Spatula**: A steel or wooden spatula ensures no food is wasted.
- **Baby Food Maker (Optional)**: Multi-function baby food makers combine steaming and blending. While convenient, they're not essential if you have a pressure cooker and mixer grinder.
- **Measuring tools**: Use measuring tools for the accurate measurements of ingredients, for example, measuring spoon sets, measuring cup sets etc.,

2.2. Food Safety Guidelines

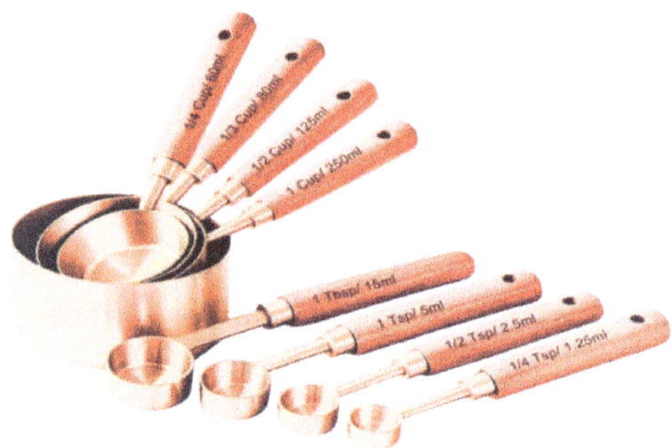

Food safety is paramount when preparing baby food, as infants have developing immune systems. Follow these guidelines to minimize risks:

- **Hygiene:**
    - Wash hands with soap for at least 20 seconds before handling food or equipment, reducing bacterial contamination by up to 99%.
    - Clean all tools, cutting boards, and countertops with hot soapy water. In Indian households, boiling water can be used to sterilize utensils.
    - Rinse fruits and vegetables thoroughly under running water, even if peeling, to remove dirt and pesticide residues. For leafy greens like spinach (palak), soak in water with a pinch of salt or vinegar for 5 minutes to dislodge contaminants.

- **Storage:**

Storage of baby food is not an ideal practice; however, in the world of buzz, refrigeration of purees and other baby foods is practiced, which is not recommended unless left with situations with no other go. In such unavoidable situations, refrigerate purees within 2 hours of preparation to prevent bacterial growth (e.g., Bacillus cereus, common in rice-based purees). Use within 48 hours at 4°C or lower.

- **Avoiding Choking Hazards:**
    - Ensure age-appropriate textures: smooth purees for 6–8 months, thicker purees for 9–12 months, and soft finger foods for 9+ months, aligning with developmental milestones.
    - Avoid high-risk foods like whole grapes, nuts, raw carrots, or sticky foods (e.g., jaggery balls) until age 4, as they pose choking risks due to underdeveloped swallowing reflexes.
    - Always supervise feeding, ensuring the baby is seated upright to minimize aspiration risks (baby can also be secured on a high chair under the supervision of a caregiver).

2.3. Tips for Selecting Fresh, Organic, and Seasonal Ingredients

Choosing high-quality ingredients ensures optimal nutrition and flavour. Here's how to select ingredients suited for Indian markets:

- **Freshness**: Opt for firm, vibrant produce without bruises, mold, or soft spots. Shop at local mandis or sabzi markets for fresher options compared to supermarkets. For example, choose bright green spinach or firm, glossy bottle gourds. Fresh produce retains higher nutrient levels (e.g., vitamin A in carrots degrades with prolonged storage).
- **Organic**: Organic produce minimizes exposure to pesticides, critical for infants with sensitive systems. Prioritize organic for thin-skinned fruits and vegetables (e.g., apples, tomatoes, spinach), as they absorb more pesticides. In India, look for NPOP (National Programme for Organic Production) certified organic brands or local farmers practicing natural farming. If budget-constrained, rinse non-organic produce thoroughly or peel where possible.

How To Choose Organic Products

Hindi Logo English Logo

Just like green & red dots on products to signify if they are vegetarian or non-vegetarian, the Food Safety and Standards Authority of India (FSSAI) in December 2017, introduced the Jaivik Bharat logo to help customers identify authentic organic food.

Additionally, all four logos are valid for Indian consumers. The blue and red 'India Organic' logo indicates that the product is officially certified organic. The PGS-India Green logo shows that the product comes from farms transitioning to organic, having stopped using chemicals. The PGS-India Organic logo means the product comes from farms that completed the organic conversion and are fully certified as organic. The USDA Organic logo confirms that the product is organic and meets export standards for the US. Any of these logos on a product guarantees its v.

Therefore, if you find any of the above logos on a product of your choice, you can rest assured that the product is not fake. Some products feature the logos either on the front, sides, or the back of the package - look for them.

- **Seasonal**: Seasonal produce is fresher, tastier, and more affordable.
- **Variety**: Introduce a range of colors and nutrients to support growth. For example, orange vegetables (carrots, pumpkin) provide beta-carotene, green leafy vegetables (spinach) offer iron, and fruits like bananas provide potassium. Rotate ingredients to expose babies to diverse flavours and colours, reducing picky eating later.

3: First Foods (6-8 Months) - A Flavourful Start for Your Little Foodie

Welcome to Your Baby's Food Adventure

Introducing solids to your 6- to 8-month-old is an exciting milestone, marking their first steps into a world of flavours and textures. This stage is an opportunity to create nutrient-rich, homemade purees that support your baby's growth and ignite their curiosity. This chapter explores the magic of single- and double-ingredient purees, gives tips for safely introducing allergens, and offers practical feeding schedules and portion sizes tailored for parents.

3.1. Importance of Single-Ingredient Purees - The Building Blocks of Taste

At 6–8 months, your baby's digestive system is ready for solids as the tongue-thrust reflex fades, and their oral motor skills begin to blossom. Single-ingredient purees are the perfect starting point, offering a gentle introduction to new flavours while keeping things safe and simple. Here's why they're a game-changer:

> **Tip:** Diced steamed vegetables (beetroot, carrot, sweet potato) support self-feeding and motor skill development.

- **Flavour Exploration**: Each puree introduces a distinct taste, helping your baby accept diverse flavours early, which can reduce picky eating later. Think of it as laying the foundation for a lifelong love of spices and ingredients.
- **Nutritional Powerhouse**: These purees deliver critical nutrients which becomes essential at 6 months and after, supporting brain and muscle development.
- **Texture Perfection**: Silky, lump-free purees are ideal for early eaters, preventing choking and supporting the development of swallowing and spoon-feeding skills.

3.2. Preparation Tips for Perfect Purees

- **Maximize Nutrients**: Steam ingredients to preserve vital nutrients. A pressure cooker, a staple in Indian kitchens, along with a steamer basket, is perfect for quick steaming.
- **Smooth Consistency**: Blend with breast milk, formula, or boiled water to create a thin, silky texture that's easy for your baby to swallow.
- **Hygiene First**: Wash hands, utensils, and ingredients thoroughly. Sterilize utensils with boiling water.

3.3. Delicious First Food Recipes

These recipes are designed for parents, using locally available ingredients and straightforward methods. Each recipe (1–2 tablespoons) provides small portions. They aim to be nutrient-dense, simple to make, and full of flavours your baby will enjoy.

🛠 **Kitchen Hack:** Use a mixer grinder for blending and a fine mesh strainer to strain out any fibrous bits, ensuring a smooth puree.

3.3.1. Mashed Banana Delight

Ingredients:

- ½ ripe banana (yellow with no green)
- 1–2 tbsp breast milk, formula, or boiled water (optional, for thinning)

Instructions:

1. Peel the banana and cut it into small pieces for easy mashing.
2. Mash with a fork or blend in a mixer grinder for a smoother texture.
3. Add breast milk, formula, or boiled water to achieve a thin, spoonable consistency.
4. Serve fresh for the best flavour and texture.

Nutritional Benefits: High in potassium for muscle function and carbohydrates for energy. Its soft texture and mild sweetness make it a perfect first food.

Tip: Elaichi bananas (small, sweet) are widely available and perfect for babies. Avoid overripe ones with black spots.

3.3.2. Papaya Puree

Ingredients:

- Fresh Papaya (sweet variety - 20 to 30 grams)
- 1-2 tbsp breast milk, formula, or boiled water (optional, for thinning)

Instructions:

1. Wash, peel, core, and chop the papaya into small pieces.
2. Mash with a fork or blend in a mixer grinder for a smoother texture.
3. Add breast milk, formula, or boiled water to achieve a thin, spoonable consistency.
4. Serve fresh for the best flavour and texture.

> 💡 **Tip:** Source seasonal papayas for freshness and sweetness.

Nutritional Benefits: Rich in vitamin C for immunity and natural sugars for energy. Gentle on the stomach, making it ideal for sensitive tummies.

3.3.3. Creamy Avocado Mash

Ingredients:

- 1 ripe avocado (soft when gently squeezed, no brown spots)
- 1–2 tbsp breast milk, formula, or boiled water (optional, for thinning)

Instructions:

1. Slice the avocado in half, remove the pit, and scoop out the creamy flesh with a spoon.
2. Mash with a fork or blend in a mixer grinder until velvety smooth.
3. Add breast milk, formula, or boiled water to achieve a thin, spoonable consistency.
4. Serve immediately to maintain freshness and prevent browning.

💡 **Tip:** Choose ripe ones for immediate use, and check for firmness to avoid overripe fruit.

Nutritional Benefits: Packed with monounsaturated fats for brain development and energy, plus vitamin E for healthy skin and immunity.

3.3.4. Sweet Potato Puree

Ingredients:

- 1 medium sweet potato (100 - 150 g)
- 2-3 tbsp breast milk, formula, or boiled water (optional, for thinning)

🛠**Kitchen Hack:** Strain through a fine channi for an extra-smooth texture, if needed.

Instructions:

1. Wash, peel, and chop the sweet potato into small cubes for even cooking.
2. Steam in a pressure cooker (1 - 2 whistles) or steamer for 10-12 minutes until fork-tender.
3. Blend in a mixer grinder with boiled water or breast milk until smooth.

💡 **Tip:** Select firm ones with smooth, unblemished skin for the best flavour and nutrient content.

Nutritional Benefits: Loaded with beta-carotene (vitamin A) for vision and immunity, fiber for digestion, and carbohydrates for energy.

3.3.5. Pear Mash

Ingredients:

- ½ ripe pear (soft, no green skin)
- 1–2 tbsp breast milk, formula, or boiled water (optional, for thinning)

Tip: Choose ripe, juicy pears for natural sweetness. Ensure no hard bits remain to avoid choking hazards.

Instructions:

1. Wash, peel, and core the pear, then cut it into small chunks.
2. Steam the pear pieces for 5–7 minutes until soft.
3. Mash with a fork or blend in a mixer grinder for a smoother texture.
4. Add breast milk, formula, or boiled water to achieve a thin, spoonable consistency.
5. Serve fresh for the best flavour.

Nutritional Benefits: High in fiber for digestion, vitamin C for immunity, and antioxidants. Its mild flavour and soft texture make it ideal for early weaning.

3.3.6. Pumpkin Puree

Ingredients:

- ½ cup pumpkin (peeled and cubed, about 100g)
- 2-3 tbsp breast milk, formula, or boiled water (optional, for thinning)

💡 **Tip:** Use good-quality pumpkin for a creamier texture.

Instructions:

1. Wash, peel, and cube the pumpkin into small pieces.
2. Steam for 10-15 minutes until tender.
3. Blend in a mixer grinder or mash with a fork for a smooth texture.
4. Add breast milk, formula, or boiled water to achieve a spoonable consistency.
5. Serve fresh for optimal taste.

Nutritional Benefits: Rich in vitamin A (beta-carotene) for eye health, vitamin C for immunity, and fiber for digestion.

3.3.7. Carrot Puree

Ingredients:

- 1 medium carrot (about 100–120g, fresh and firm)
- 2–3 tbsp breast milk, formula, or boiled water (optional, for thinning)

Tip: Choose bright orange carrots for higher beta-carotene.

Instructions:

1. Wash, peel, and chop the carrot into small chunks.
2. Steam for 10–12 minutes until soft.
3. Blend in a mixer grinder or mash thoroughly for a smooth texture.
4. Add breast milk, formula, or boiled water to achieve a thin, spoonable consistency.
5. Serve fresh for the best flavour and nutrient retention.

Nutritional Benefits: High in vitamin A for eye health and immunity, plus fiber for digestion.

3.3.8. Bottle Gourd Puree

Ingredients:

- ½ cup bottle gourd (peeled and cubed, about 100g)
- 2-3 tbsp breast milk, formula, or boiled water (optional, for thinning)

Tip: Ensure the bottle gourd is tender and not bitter (taste before cooking).

Instructions:

1. Wash, peel, and chop the bottle gourd into small pieces.
2. Steam for 8-10 minutes until very soft.
3. Blend in a mixer grinder or mash with a fork for a smooth texture.
4. Add breast milk, formula, or boiled water to achieve a thin consistency.
5. Serve fresh to avoid any bitterness.

Nutritional Benefits: Hydrating and easy to digest, rich in vitamins C and B. Its mild flavour is perfect for early weaning.

3.3.9. Ragi Porridge

Ingredients:

- 1–2 tbsp ragi (finger millet) flour
- 1 cup water or breast milk/formula (for cooking)
- 1–2 tbsp breast milk or formula (optional, for flavour and thinning)

> **Tip:** Add mashed fruit (like banana) for sweetness, but avoid sugar or honey for babies under 1 year.

Instructions:

1. Mix ragi flour with 2–3 tbsp water to form a smooth paste, avoiding lumps.
2. Heat 1 cup water in a small pan on low heat, then slowly stir in the ragi paste.
3. Cook for 5–7 minutes, stirring continuously to prevent lumps, until it thickens to a porridge-like consistency.
4. Cool slightly, then add breast milk or formula for a creamier texture, if desired.
5. Serve warm in a small bowl and spoon-feed.

Nutritional Benefits: Rich in calcium for bone development, iron for blood health, and fiber for digestion. Provides sustained energy, making it ideal for growing babies.

3.3.10. Moong Dal Porridge

Ingredients:

- 1–2 tbsp moong dal (split yellow lentils, soaked for 1–2 hours)
- 1 cup water (for cooking)
- 1–2 tbsp breast milk or formula (optional, for thinning)

Tip: For 8+ months, add a pinch of cumin powder for flavour. Introduce dal gradually to ensure digestibility.

Instructions:

1. Rinse and soak moong dal in water for 1–2 hours, then drain the water.
2. Cook dal with 1 cup water in a small pan or pressure cooker (1 whistle) until very soft.
3. Blend or mash thoroughly to a smooth, porridge-like consistency.
4. Add breast milk, formula, or boiled water to achieve a thin, spoonable texture.
5. Serve warm for the best flavour.

Nutritional Benefits: High in protein and iron for growth and blood health, plus folate for development. Easy to digest for young tummies.

3.3.11. Apple and Pear Blend

Ingredients:

- ½ apple (sweet variety, e.g., Fuji, Gala, or Kashmiri apple)
- ½ pear (soft, ripe)
- 2–3 tbsp boiled water

Instructions:

1. Wash, peel, core, and chop the apple and pear into small pieces.
2. Steam in a pressure cooker (1-2 whistles) or steamer for 8–10 minutes until soft.

Tip: Source good-quality Pears and apples for sweetness.

3. Blend with boiled water until smooth and lump-free.
4. Cool to room temperature before serving to ensure safety.

Nutritional Benefits: Rich in vitamin C for immunity and natural sugars for energy. Gentle on the stomach, making it ideal for sensitive tummies.

3.3.12. Oats Banana Mash

Ingredients:

- 1–2 tbsp rolled oats
- ½ ripe banana (yellow, no black spots)
- ½ cup water or breast milk/formula (for cooking)

Tip: Use small, sweet bananas (like elaichi) for better flavour. Ensure oats are well-cooked for younger babies (6+ months).

Instructions:

1. Cook oats in ½ cup water on low heat for 5–7 minutes until soft.
2. Peel and mash the banana with a fork.
3. Mix the cooked oats and mashed banana, blending for a smoother texture if needed.
4. Add a splash of breast milk or formula to adjust consistency, if desired.
5. Serve warm or at room temperature.

Nutritional Benefits: Oats provide fiber and sustained energy; bananas add potassium and natural sweetness, supporting muscle function.

3.3.13. Oats Apple Puree

Ingredients:

- 1–2 tbsp rolled oats
- ½ apple (peeled and cored)
- ½ cup water or breast milk/formula (for cooking)

Instructions:

1. Wash, peel, and core the apple, then chop it into small pieces.
2. Steam apple pieces for 8–10 minutes until soft.
3. Cook oats in ½ cup water on low heat for 5–7 minutes until soft.
4. Blend steamed apple and cooked oats for a smooth texture.
5. Add breast milk, formula, or water to achieve a spoonable consistency. Serve warm.

💡 **Tip: Source good-quality apples for natural sweetness.**

Nutritional Benefit22s: Apples provide fiber and vitamin C for digestion and immunity; oats add energy and fiber for satiety.

3.3.14. Oats Carrot Puree

Ingredients:

- 1–2 tbsp rolled oats
- 1 small carrot (about 80–100g, peeled)
- ½ cup water or breast milk/formula (for cooking)

Instructions:

1. Wash, peel, and chop the carrot into small chunks.
2. Steam carrots for 10–12 minutes until tender.
3. Cook oats in ½ cup water on low heat for 5–7 minutes until soft.
4. Blend steamed carrots and cooked oats for a smooth puree.
5. Add breast milk, formula, or water to achieve a thin, spoonable consistency. Serve warm.

Tip: Ensure carrots are fully steamed for easy blending. For 8+ months, a pinch of cinnamon can be added to enhance flavour.

Nutritional Benefits: Carrots provide vitamin A for eye health; oats add fiber and energy, making this a balanced meal for babies.

3.3.15. Mango and Rice Puree

Ingredients:

- 1/2 ripe mango
- 2 tbsp cooked rice
- 2–3 tbsp boiled water

Tip: Use seasonal mangoes for natural sweetness. Source from local markets in summer.

Instructions:

1. Scoop the pulp of the ripe mango.
2. Blend with cooked rice and boiled water to a smooth, thick puree.
3. Cool to room temperature before serving.

Nutritional Benefits: Mango provides vitamin C and A for immunity and vision, while rice offers carbohydrates for energy.

Tip: Offer water (1–2 tsp) with a spoon or in a lidless cup during meals to introduce sipping skills, avoiding sugary drinks like fruit juices.

3.4. Portion Sizes

- Start with 1-2 tsp per meal, gradually increasing to 2–4 tbsp as your baby accepts solids.
- By 8 months, a typical serving is 1/4–1/2 cup (60–120 ml) per meal, depending on appetite.
- Let your baby guide portion sizes; avoid force-feeding to prevent feeding aversions.

Just a Sample Daily Schedule (6–8 Months)

- 7:00 AM: Breast milk/formula (150–200 ml)
- 10:00 AM: 2–4 tbsp sweet potato puree + breast milk/formula (100 ml)
- 1:00 PM: Breast milk/formula (150–200 ml)
- 4:00 PM: 2–4 tbsp apple-pear blend + breast milk/formula (100 ml)
- 7:00 PM: Breast milk/formula (150–200 ml)
- Night: Breast milk/formula on demand

4: Textured Blends (8-10 Months) - Transitioning to Thicker Purees & Simple Food Combinations

Welcome to Your Baby's Flavourful Leap Forward

At 8–10 months, your baby is ready to transition to thicker textures and more exciting flavour combinations, marking a vibrant phase in their culinary journey. In Indian households, where food is a celebration of culture and connection, this stage allows you to introduce nutrient-packed, homemade blends that support your baby's growing curiosity and developmental needs. This chapter explores the transition to thicker purees and simple food combinations, offers Indian-inspired recipes, provides guidance on introducing mild spices and herbs, and encourages self-feeding with soft finger foods.

4.1. Importance of Thicker Purees and Simple Food Combinations?

Between 8 and 10 months, your baby's oral motor skills improve, with stronger gums and developing chewing abilities, even without teeth. Thicker purees and simple food combinations introduce new textures and flavours, supporting jaw development and sensory exploration. These combinations also offer balanced nutrition, combining vitamins, minerals, and proteins to promote physical and cognitive growth. Here

> **Allergy Safety:** Combining familiar foods with new ones allows continued vigilance for allergic reactions, maintaining a 2–3 day gap for new ingredients.

- **Texture Progression**: Thicker purees and mashed foods encourage chewing, strengthening jaw muscles, and preparing babies for finger foods.
- **Nutritional Synergy**: Pairing ingredients enhances nutrient absorption, such as vitamin C, boosting iron uptake, critical for brain and muscle development.
- **Flavour Development**: Combining foods introduces complex tastes, encouraging acceptance of diverse Indian flavours and reducing picky eating later.

4.2. Importance of Introducing Mild Spices and Herbs

Mild spices and herbs can enhance flavour and stimulate sensory and cognitive development. They also expose babies to cultural tastes, encouraging acceptance of family meals later.

- **Safe Spices and Herbs:**
  - **Cumin (Jeera)**: A pinch of roasted cumin powder adds warmth to lentil or vegetable purees, and aids in the digestion of food in sensitive tummies.
  - **Cinnamon (Dalchini)**: A dash in fruit purees like apple enhances sweetness naturally.
  - **Coriander (Dhania)**: Fresh coriander leaves, finely blended, add a mild, fresh flavour.
  - **Mint (Pudina)**: A small amount of fresh mint (blended) in pea purees aids digestion and adds freshness.

> **Tip:** Source good-quality spices from local markets or trusted organic brands. Roast whole spices lightly to reduce intensity for babies.

- **Introduction Tips:**
  - Start with a tiny pinch (1/16 tsp) to avoid overwhelming your baby's palate.
  - Introduce one spice/herb at a time, waiting 2-3 days to monitor for reactions.
  - Avoid spicy or pungent spices (e.g., chili, black pepper) and salt, as they can harm developing kidneys.
  - Use fresh or lightly roasted spices for milder flavour and better nutrient retention.

4.3. Preparation Tips

- **Texture Adjustment**: Blend to a slightly thicker, mashed consistency, leaving tiny soft lumps to encourage chewing. Use a fork or mixer grinder for control.
- **Cooking Methods**: Steam or pressure-cook ingredients to preserve nutrients.
- **Hygiene**: Wash hands, utensils, and ingredients thoroughly. Sterilize with boiling water to prevent bacterial growth.

> 🛠️**Kitchen Hack:** Use a pressure cooker with a steamer basket for quick cooking, and a fine channi to strain fibrous bits if needed.

4.4. Wholesome Flavourful Combination Recipes

Below are the recipes designed using combination of ingredients and simple methods. These recipes balance nutrition and flavour, introducing your baby to the vibrant tastes of Indian cuisine.

4.4.1. Carrot Beetroot Puree

Ingredients:

- 1 small carrot (about 80–100g, peeled)
- ¼ small beetroot (about 30–40g, peeled)
- 2–3 tbsp breast milk, formula, or boiled water (optional, for thinning)

Tip: Use a small amount of beetroot to avoid overpowering flavour and monitor for allergies

Instructions:

1. Wash, peel, and chop the carrot and beetroot into small chunks.
2. Steam both together for 10–12 minutes until soft.
3. Blend into a smooth puree using a mixer grinder.
4. Add breast milk, formula, or boiled water to achieve a thin, spoonable consistency.
5. Serve fresh for the best flavour and color.

Nutritional Benefits: Carrots offer vitamin A; beetroots provide iron, folate, and antioxidants, supporting blood health and immunity.

4.4.2. Spinach and Pea Puree

Ingredients:

- 1 cup fresh spinach (palak), washed thoroughly
- 1/2 cup peas (matar), fresh
- 2-3 tbsp boiled water or breast milk

Instructions:

1. Steam spinach and peas in a pressure cooker (1-2 whistles) or steamer for 8–10 minutes until tender.
2. Blend with boiled water or breast milk to a thick, smooth puree.
3. Strain through a channi if needed for a finer texture.

Tip: Source fresh spinach and peas from local mandis, especially in winter. Soak spinach in water with a pinch of salt to remove dirt.

Nutritional Benefits: Spinach supplies iron and folate for cognitive development, while peas offer vitamin C and fiber for digestion. The combination enhances iron absorption.

4.4.3. Carrot and Lentil Mash

Ingredients:

- 1 medium carrot (80-100 g), peeled and chopped
- 2 tbsp moong dal (split yellow lentils), rinsed
- 1 cup water
- 1 tsp ghee (optional, for flavour)

Tip: Choose bright orange carrots for maximum beta-carotene.

Instructions:

1. Pressure-cook carrot and moong dal with water (1-2 whistles) or boil until soft, about 15 minutes.
2. Blend in a mixer grinder to a thick, slightly lumpy purée.
3. Stir in ghee for flavour, if desired, and cool to room temperature.

Nutritional Benefits: Carrots provide beta-carotene (vitamin A) for vision and immunity, while moong dal offers iron and protein for muscle and brain growth. Ghee adds healthy fats for energy.

4.4.4. Oatmeal Mango Mash

Ingredients:

- 2 tbsp rolled oats
- 1/2 cup water
- 1/4 cup fresh blueberries

Tip: Substitute with blueberry (steamed) for a seasonal twist.

Instructions:

1. Cook the oats in water over low heat for 5–7 minutes, stirring until they have thickened.
2. Take the pulp of the ripe mango and mash or blend.
3. Mix mashed mango into oatmeal for a thick, textured mix.

Nutritional Benefits: Oats provide carbohydrates and fiber for energy and digestion, while Mango provides vitamin C and A for immunity and vision.

4.4.5. Ragi Banana Halwa

Ingredients:

- 2 tbsp ragi (finger millet) flour
- ½ ripe banana (yellow, no black spots)
- ¾ cup water (for cooking)
- 1 tsp ghee (optional)
- 1–2 tbsp breast milk or formula (optional, for thinning)

Tip: Use small, sweet bananas (like elaichi) for better flavour. Ensure ragi is well-cooked to avoid graininess, especially for younger babies.

Instructions:

1. Mix ragi flour with ¼ cup water to form a smooth paste, avoiding lumps.
2. Heat ½ cup of water in a small pan on low heat, then slowly stir in the ragi paste.
3. Cook for 5–7 minutes, stirring continuously, until it thickens to a halwa-like consistency.
4. Peel and mash the banana thoroughly, then mix it into the cooked ragi. Add ghee (if using) for richness and stir well.
5. Add breast milk or formula to adjust consistency. Cool and serve warm.

Nutritional Benefits: Ragi is high in calcium and iron for bone and blood health; banana provides potassium and natural sweetness for energy. Ghee (if used) adds healthy fats for brain development.

4.4.6. Jowar Mango Halwa

Ingredients:

- 2 tbsp jowar (sorghum) flour
- ½ ripe mango
  (sweet variety, peeled and pureed)
- ¾ cup water (for cooking)
- 1 tsp ghee (optional)
- 1–2 tbsp breast milk or formula (optional, for thinning)

Tip: Use ripe, non-fibrous mangoes for better taste.

Instructions:

1. Mix jowar flour with ¼ cup water to form a smooth paste, avoiding lumps.
2. Heat ½ cup of water in a small pan on low heat, then slowly stir in the jowar paste.
3. Cook for 5–7 minutes, stirring continuously, until it thickens to a sheera-like consistency.
4. Add mango puree and ghee (if using), mixing well to combine.
5. Blend for a smoother texture (for 8+ months) or keep slightly thick (for 9+ months). Add breast milk or formula to adjust consistency. Cool and serve warm.

Nutritional Benefits: Jowar provides iron, fiber, and antioxidants for blood health and digestion; mangoes offer vitamins A and C for immunity and natural sweetness.

4.4.7. Carrot Kheer

Ingredients:

- ¼ cup carrot (peeled, finely grated)
- 1 tbsp rice (preferably regional, rinsed)
- ½ cup coconut milk (for cooking)
- ½ tsp ghee (optional)
- Pinch of cardamom powder (optional)

💡 **Tip:** Use homemade coconut milk for safety. For 9+ months, serve slightly thicker to encourage spoon-feeding.

Instructions:

1. Steam grated carrot for 5-7 minutes until soft, then mash or blend finely.
2. Rinse rice, soak for 1-2 hours, then cook with ½ cup water in a small pan for 5-7 minutes until soft and mushy.
3. Add mashed carrot and coconut milk to the cooked rice, stirring on low heat for 3-4 minutes until creamy.
4. Add ghee and cardamom powder (if using), mixing well.
5. Blend for a smooth texture or keep slightly textured (9+ months). Cool to a safe temperature and serve warm.

Nutritional Benefits: Carrots provide vitamin A and fiber for immunity and digestion; rice offers carbohydrates for energy; coconut milk adds creaminess and nutrients. Ghee (if used) supports brain development.

4.4.8. Makhana Kheer

Ingredients:

- 2 tbsp makhana (fox nuts, whole)
- ½ cup coconut milk (thin, homemade, ensure no additives)
- 1 tbsp rice (preferably regional, rinsed)
- 1–2 tbsp breast milk or formula (optional, for thinning)
- Pinch of cardamom powder (optional)

Tip: Test coconut milk and makhana separately for allergies. For 9+ months, a small amount of mashed banana can enhance sweetness.

Instructions:

1. Dry roast makhana on low heat for 5–7 minutes until crisp. Cool and grind into a coarse powder.
2. Rinse rice thoroughly, soak for 1–2 hours, then drain.
3. Cook rice with ½ cup water in a small pan on low heat for 5–7 minutes until soft.
4. Add makhana powder and coconut milk, stirring for 3–5 minutes until it forms a creamy kheer. Add cardamom powder, if using.
5. Blend for a smooth texture or keep slightly grainy (for 9+ months). Add breast milk or formula to adjust consistency. Cool and serve warm.

Nutritional Benefits: Makhana provides protein and magnesium for growth; coconut milk offers healthy fats for brain development; rice adds digestible carbohydrates for energy.

4.4.9. Steamed Apple with Nuts and Seeds Powder

Ingredients:

- ½ apple (fresh, peeled and cored)
- 1 tsp mixed nuts and seeds powder (2 almonds, 2 cashews, 1 tsp pumpkin seeds)
- 1–2 tbsp breast milk or formula (optional, for thinning)
- Pinch of cinnamon powder (optional)

Instructions:

1. Wash, peel, and core the apple, then chop it into small pieces.
2. Steam the apple pieces for 8–10 minutes until soft.
3. Dry roast almonds, cashews, and pumpkin seeds separately on low heat for 2–3 minutes until fragrant. Cool and grind into a fine powder using a mixer grinder. Sieve for smoothness.
4. Mash or blend the steamed apple into a smooth puree, then stir in 1 teaspoon of the nuts and seeds powder and cinnamon (if using)..
5. Add breast milk or formula to achieve a thin, spoonable consistency. Cool to a safe temperature and serve.

Tip: Introduce nuts and seeds individually for 3 days to check for allergies, as they are potential allergens. Start with a small amount (½ tsp powder) for 8+ months.

Nutritional Benefits: Apples provide fiber and vitamin C for digestion and immunity; nuts and seeds offer healthy fats, protein, and minerals (like magnesium) for brain and bone health. Cinnamon adds a mild flavour and antioxidants.

4.4.10. Dalia Porridge

Ingredients:

- 2 tbsp dalia (broken wheat, rinsed)
- 1 tbsp moong dal (split yellow lentils, rinsed)
- 1 cup water (for cooking)
- 1–2 tbsp breast milk or formula (optional, for thinning and flavour)

Instructions:

💡 **Tip: Add a pinch of cumin powder for flavour enhancement.**

1. Wash dalia and moong dal thoroughly. Soak for 1–2 hours, then drain.
2. Pressure cook dalia and moong dal with 1 cup of water for 2-3 whistles, until the mixture is soft and porridge-like.
3. Now, blend the mixture to a smooth consistency using a mixer grinder.
4. Add breast milk or formula to achieve a thin, spoonable texture, if desired.
5. Cool to a safe temperature and serve warm.

Nutritional Benefits: Dalia provides complex carbohydrates and fiber for sustained energy and digestion; moong dal adds protein and iron for growth. Rich in B vitamins for metabolism.

4.4.11. Dalia Porridge with Veggies

Ingredients:

- 2 tbsp dalia
  (broken wheat, rinsed)
- 1 tbsp moong dal
  (split yellow lentils, rinsed)
- ¼ cup mixed veggies (carrot and peas, finely chopped)
- ¾ cup water (for cooking)
- 1 tsp ghee (optional)

Tip: Add a pinch of cumin powder for flavour enhancement.

Instructions:

1. Rinse dalia and moong dal thoroughly, soak for 1–2 hours, then drain.
2. Steam carrots and peas for 5–7 minutes until soft, then mash or blend finely.
3. In a small pan or pressure cooker, cook dalia and moong dal with ¾ cup water for 10–12 minutes until soft.
4. Mix in mashed veggies and ghee (if using), stirring well.
5. Blend to a smooth consistency for younger babies or keep slightly textured for older ones. Cool and serve warm.

Nutritional Benefits: Dalia provides fiber and energy; moong dal adds protein and iron; veggies offer vitamins A and C for immunity and growth.

4.4.12. Little Millet and Makhana Porridge

Ingredients:

- 1 tbsp little millet (samai, rinsed)
- 1 tbsp makhana (fox nuts, whole)
- 1 cup water (for cooking)
- 1–2 tbsp breast milk or formula (optional, for thinning)
- Pinch of cardamom powder (optional)

Instructions:

1. Rinse little millet thoroughly and soak for 1–2 hours, then drain.
2. Dry roast makhana on low heat for 3–4 minutes until crisp. Cool and grind into a coarse powder.
3. In a small pan, cook little millet with 1 cup of water on low heat for 8–10 minutes until soft.
4. Add makhana powder and stir for 2–3 minutes to combine. Add a pinch of cardamom powder, if using.
5. Blend for a smoother texture (for 8+ months) or keep slightly grainy (for 9+ months). Add breast milk or formula to adjust consistency. Cool and serve warm.

💡 **Tip:** For 9+ months, add a pinch of cumin powder for flavour.

Nutritional Benefits: Little millet is rich in iron, magnesium, and fiber for blood health and digestion; makhana provides protein and antioxidants. Adding cardamom powder in small amounts aids digestion.

4.4.13. Amaranth Porridge

Tip: Start with a small serving (½ tsp) to ensure digestibility. Can mix with mashed apple for variety.

Ingredients:

- 2 tbsp amaranth flour or grains (rinsed if using grains)
- 1 cup water (for cooking)
- 1–2 tbsp breast milk or formula (optional, for thinning)
- ½ tsp mashed banana

Instructions:

1. If using amaranth grains, rinse and soak for 2 hours, then drain. If using flour, skip soaking.
2. In a small pan, cook amaranth (grains or flour) with 1 cup water on low heat for 8–10 minutes, stirring continuously to avoid lumps, until it forms a smooth porridge.
3. Add mashed banana (if using) for natural sweetness and stir well.
4. Blend for a smoother texture (for 8+ months) or keep slightly grainy (for 9+ months). Add breast milk or formula to adjust consistency.
5. Cool and serve warm.

Nutritional Benefits: Amaranth is high in protein, calcium, and iron for growth and bone health; banana adds potassium and sweetness for energy and digestion.

4.4.14. Barnyard Millet Khichdi

Ingredients:

- 2 tbsp barnyard millet (sanwa, rinsed)
- 1 tbsp moong dal (split yellow lentils, rinsed)
- 1 cup water (for cooking)
- 1 tsp ghee (optional)
- Pinch of cumin powder (optional)

Tip: For 9+ months, add mashed vegetables like carrots for added nutrition.

Instructions:

1. Rinse barnyard millet and moong dal thoroughly, soak for 1-2 hours, then drain.
2. In a small pan, cook millet and dal with 1 cup of water on low heat for 10-12 minutes until soft and mushy.
3. Add ghee and cumin powder (if using) and stir well.
4. Blend to a smooth consistency for younger babies or keep slightly textured for older ones.
5. Cool to a safe temperature and serve warm.
6. **Nutritional Benefits**: Barnyard millet is rich in fiber and B vitamins for digestion and energy; moong dal provides protein and iron for growth. Ghee adds healthy fats.

4.4.15. Pearl Millet Khichdi

Ingredients:

- 2 tbsp bajra (pearl millet, rinsed)
- 1 tbsp moong dal (split yellow lentils, rinsed)
- ¼ cup spinach (finely chopped, washed thoroughly)
- 1½ cup water (for cooking)
- 1 tsp ghee (optional)

Tip: Ensure spinach is well-cooked and finely blended to avoid choking.

Instructions:

1. Rinse bajra and moong dal, soak for 2–3 hours, then drain.
2. Pressure cook bajra and dal with 1½ cups of water on low heat for 5–7 whistles until soft.
3. Steam spinach separately for 3–4 minutes until wilted, then blend or mash finely.
4. Mix spinach into the cooked millet-dal mixture, add ghee (if using), and stir well.
5. Blend for a smooth texture (8+ months) or keep slightly chunky (9+ months). Cool and serve warm.

Nutritional Benefits: Bajra provides iron and fiber for blood health and digestion; spinach is rich in vitamins A and C for immunity; moong dal adds protein.

4.4.16. Little Millet Khichdi

Ingredients:

- 2 tbsp little millet (samai, rinsed)
- 1 tbsp moong dal (split yellow lentils, rinsed)
- 1 cup water (for cooking)
- ¼ cup carrot (peeled, finely chopped, optional)
- 1 tsp ghee (optional)

Tip: For 9+ months, add mashed peas for extra nutrition after confirming no allergies.

Instructions:

1. Rinse little millet and moong dal thoroughly, soak for 1–2 hours, then drain.
2. In a small pan or pressure cooker, cook millet and dal with 1 cup water (and carrot, if using) on low heat for 10–12 minutes (or 2-3 whistles in a pressure cooker) until soft and mushy.
3. Add ghee (if using) and stir well to combine.
4. Blend to a smooth consistency for younger babies or keep slightly textured for older ones.
5. Cool to a safe temperature and serve warm.

Nutritional Benefits: Little millet provides fiber, iron, and B vitamins for digestion and energy; moong dal adds protein and iron for growth; carrots offer vitamin A for immunity.

4.4.17. Foxtail Millet Khichdi

Ingredients:

- 1 tbsp foxtail millet (rinsed)
- 1 tbsp moong dal (split yellow lentils, rinsed)
- ½ cup water (for cooking)
- ¼ cup mashed pumpkin (optional)
- 1 tsp ghee (optional)

Tip: For 9+ months, add mashed spinach for extra nutrients.

Instructions:

1. Rinse foxtail millet and moong dal thoroughly, soak for 1–2 hours, then drain.
2. In a small pan or pressure cooker, cook millet and dal with ½ cup water (and pumpkin, if using) on low heat for 10–12 minutes (or 2-3 whistles) until soft and mushy.
3. Add ghee (if using) and stir well.
4. Blend to a smooth consistency for younger babies or keep slightly textured for older ones.
5. Cool to a safe temperature and serve warm.

Nutritional Benefits: Foxtail millet offers fiber and B vitamins for energy; moong dal provides protein and iron for growth; pumpkin adds vitamin A for immunity.

4.4.18. Suji Upma

Ingredients:

- 2 tbsp suji (semolina, fine variety, roasted)
- ¼ cup mixed vegetables (carrot and peas, finely chopped)
- ¾ cup water (for cooking)
- 1 tsp ghee (optional)
- Pinch of roasted cumin powder (optional)

Instructions:

1. Dry roast suji in a pan on low heat for 2–3 minutes until lightly fragrant, if not pre-roasted. Set aside.
2. Steam carrots and peas for 5–7 minutes until soft, then mash or blend finely for younger babies.
3. In a small pan, heat ¾ cup of water, add roasted suji slowly, and stir continuously to avoid lumps.
4. Cook on low heat for 5–7 minutes until it forms a soft, porridge-like consistency. Add mashed vegetables and ghee (if using), stirring well.
5. Blend for a smoother texture or keep slightly textured (9+ months). Add cumin powder (if using) for a mild flavour. Cool and serve warm.

Tip: Ensure vegetables are well-cooked and soft to avoid choking. For 9+ months, serve as a soft finger food to encourage self-feeding.

Nutritional Benefits: Suji provides carbohydrates for energy; carrots and peas offer vitamin A, fiber, and antioxidants for immunity and digestion. Ghee (if used) adds healthy fats for brain development.

4.4.19. Spinach Rice

Ingredients:

- 2 tbsp rice (preferably regional rice, rinsed)
- ¼ cup spinach (finely chopped, washed thoroughly)
- ¾ cup water (for cooking)
- 1 tsp ghee (optional, for 8+ months)

Instructions:

1. Rinse rice thoroughly and soak for 1–2 hours, then drain.
2. Steam spinach separately for 3–4 minutes until wilted, then blend or mash finely.
3. Cook rice with ¾ cup water in a small pan or pressure cooker for 5–7 minutes until soft.
4. Mix in spinach puree and ghee (if using), stirring well to combine.
5. Blend for a smooth texture (8+ months) or keep slightly chunky (9+ months). Cool and serve warm.

Tip: Ensure spinach is well-cooked and finely blended to avoid choking.

Nutritional Benefits: Spinach is rich in iron and vitamins A and C for blood health and immunity; rice provides digestible carbohydrates for energy.

4.4.20. Carrot Rice

Ingredients:

- 2 tbsp rice (preferably regional rice, rinsed)
- ¼ cup carrot (peeled, finely chopped)
- ¾ cup water (for cooking)
- 1 tsp ghee (optional)

> **Tip:** Use bright orange carrots for higher beta-carotene.

Instructions:

1. Rinse rice thoroughly and soak for 1–2 hours, then drain.
2. Steam carrot pieces for 5–7 minutes until soft, then mash or blend finely.
3. Cook rice with ¾ cup water in a small pan or pressure cooker for 5–7 minutes until soft.
4. Mix in carrot puree and ghee (if using), stirring well.
5. Blend for a smooth texture or keep slightly chunky (9+ months). Cool and serve warm.

Nutritional Benefits: Carrots provide vitamin A for eye health and immunity; rice offers digestible carbohydrates for energy.

4.4.21. Spinach - Sweet Potato Rice Balls

Ingredients:

- 2 tbsp rice (preferably regional, rinsed)
- ¼ cup spinach (finely chopped, washed thoroughly)
- 2 tbsp mashed sweet potato (for binding)
- 1 tsp ghee (optional)

Instructions:

> **Tip:** Ensure spinach is well-cooked and finely mashed to avoid choking. Test each ingredient separately for allergies.

1. Rinse rice, soak for 1-2 hours, then cook with ½ cup water in a pan or pressure cooker for 5-7 minutes until soft. Mash lightly.
2. Steam spinach for 3-4 minutes until wilted, then mash or blend finely.
3. Steam sweet potato for 10-12 minutes, then mash thoroughly.
4. Mix mashed rice, spinach, and sweet potato to form a soft dough. Shape into small balls (1-inch diameter).
5. Optionally, lightly pan-fry with ghee on low heat for 1-2 minutes per side to firm up slightly, keeping them soft.
6. Cool to a safe temperature and serve as finger food.

Nutritional Benefits: Spinach provides iron and vitamins A and C for blood health and immunity; rice offers carbohydrates for energy; sweet potato adds fiber and vitamin A.

4.4.22. Millet Dosa

Ingredients:

- 2 tbsp little millet (samai) or foxtail millet (rinsed)
- 1 tbsp urad dal (split black gram, rinsed)
- ½ cup water (for batter and cooking)
- 1 tsp ghee (optional)

Instructions:

1. Rinse little millet and urad dal thoroughly, then soak them together in water for 4–6 hours. Drain.
2. Blend the soaked millet and dal with 2–3 tbsp water to form a smooth, slightly thin batter (like dosa batter but softer).
3. Heat a pan on low heat, lightly grease with ghee (if using).
4. Pour a small ladleful of batter (about 2 tbsp) and spread gently into a small, thick dosa (3–4 inches wide). Cook on low heat for 2-3 minutes per side until lightly golden and soft.
5. Cool slightly, cut into small pieces, or mash for younger babies. Serve warm.

💡 **Tip:** Ensure the dosa is soft and not crispy for babies.

Nutritional Benefits: Little millet provides fiber, iron, and B vitamins for energy and digestion; urad dal adds protein for growth. Ghee (if used) contributes healthy fats for brain development.

4.4.23. Baby-Friendly Pancakes

Ingredients:

- 2 tbsp oats (rolled, ground into flour)
- ½ ripe banana (yellow, no black spots)
- 2 tbsp water (for batter)
- 1 tsp ghee (optional)

> **Tip:** Cut pancakes into small, soft pieces for 9+ months to encourage self-feeding. For added flavour, mix in a tiny pinch of cinnamon.

Instructions:

1. Grind rolled oats into a fine powder using a mixer grinder.
2. Peel and mash the banana thoroughly with a fork until smooth.
3. Mix oat flour, mashed banana and water to form a smooth, slightly thick batter.
4. Heat a pan on low heat, lightly grease with ghee (if using).
5. Pour small spoonfuls of batter (1–2 tbsp each) to make mini pancakes (2–3 inches wide). Cook on low heat for 2–3 minutes per side until soft and lightly golden. Cool and serve as finger food or mash for younger babies.

Nutritional Benefits: Oats provide fiber and sustained energy; banana offers potassium and natural sweetness for muscle function and digestion. Ghee (if used) adds healthy fats.

4.5. Portion Sizes

At 8–10 months, solids become a larger part of your baby's diet, complementing breast milk or formula, which remains essential (4–5 feeds/day, 600–800 ml). Feeding schedules should align with hunger cues (e.g., reaching for food) and fullness signals (e.g., turning away).

- Start with 2–4 tbsp per meal, increasing to 1/4–1/2 cup as appetite grows.
- Let your baby guide intake; avoid force-feeding to prevent aversions.

🛠 **Kitchen Hack:** Use a pressure cooker with a steamer basket for quick cooking, and a fine channi to strain fibrous bits if needed.

Just a Sample Daily Schedule (8–10 Months)

- 7:00 AM: Breast milk/formula (150–200 ml)
- 10:00 AM: 1/4 cup Carrot-Lentil Mash + breast milk/formula (100 ml)
- 1:00 PM: Carrot Rice + Breast milk/formula (150–200 ml)
- 4:00 PM: 1/4 cup Spinach-Pea Puree + Millet Dosa + breast milk/formula (100 ml)
- 7:00 PM: Spinach Rice + Breast milk/formula (150–200 ml)
- Night: Breast milk/formula on demand

5: Textured Meals and Finger Foods (10–12 Months): Chewing, Exploring, and Dining Like a Pro

Welcome to Your Baby's Growing Appetite Adventure

At 10–12 months, your baby begins to explore as a curious, active eater, ready for chunkier textures and finger foods that nurture joy and independence. In Indian households, where meals are a lively celebration of family and flavour, this stage is an ideal time to introduce textured meals and finger foods that support your baby's developmental milestones. This section explores recipes designed to promote chewing and motor skills, offers tips for transitioning to family meals, all tailored for parents to nurture their little foodie's growth and confidence.

5.1. Importance of Chunkier Textures and Finger Foods?

Between 10 and 12 months, babies develop stronger gums, improved chewing abilities, and a refined pincer grip, enabling them to handle textured meals and finger foods. These foods promote oral motor development, enhance hand-eye coordination, and encourage self-feeding, setting the stage for lifelong healthy eating habits.

- **Oral Motor Development**: Chunky textures encourage chewing, strengthening jaw muscles, and preparing babies for complex foods.
- **Motor Skill Growth**: Grasping small, soft foods improves fine motor skills and coordination, supporting independence.
- **Nutritional Balance**: Textured meals combine proteins, carbohydrates, and vitamins to fuel rapid physical and cognitive growth.
- **Flavour Exploration**: Diverse textures and flavours reduce picky eating tendencies.

5.2. Importance of Encouraging Self-Feeding with Soft Finger Foods

At 10–12 months, babies develop fine motor skills, such as the refined pincer grip, and show interest in self-feeding. Soft finger foods encourage chewing and build confidence.

- **Tips for Self-Feeding:**
    - Offer 1–2 finger foods alongside purees at meals.
    - Supervise closely to prevent choking, ensuring babies sit upright.
    - Cut foods into small, soft pieces (no larger than 1 cm) to minimize risks.
    - Introduce finger foods gradually, starting with one type to gauge chewing ability.

> **Tip:** Use foods common in family meals to make self-feeding relevant. Involve family members during meals to encourage social engagement.

5.3. Preparation Tips

- **Texture Transition**: Aim for soft, mashed, or minced textures with small, dissolvable lumps to encourage chewing without choking risks.
- **Cooking Methods**: Steam or boil ingredients to retain nutrients. Use a pressure cooker with a steamer basket for quick prep.
- **Hygiene**: Wash hands, utensils, and ingredients thoroughly. Sterilize with boiling water to prevent bacterial growth.

> **Kitchen Hack:** Use a mixer grinder for partial blending and a fork for mashing to achieve the right texture. A pan is ideal for cooking pancakes or bites.

5.4. Recipes for Textured Meals and Finger Foods

Below are four recipes crafted for Indian parents, using accessible ingredients to create nutrient-rich, textured meals and finger foods.

5.4.1. Oats - Apple Pancake

Ingredients:

- 2 tbsp rolled oats (ground into flour)
- ¼ cup apple (peeled, grated, and steamed)
- 2–3 tbsp boiled water (for batter)
- 1 tsp ghee (optional, for cooking)

Instructions:

> 💡 Tip: Ensure fritters are soft to prevent choking.

1. Steam the grated apple for 5–7 minutes until soft, then mash lightly.
2. Grind rolled oats into a fine powder using a mixer grinder.
3. Mix oat flour, mashed apple, and add water to form a soft, thick batter.
4. Heat a pan on low heat, lightly grease with ghee (if using), and drop small spoonfuls (1 tbsp each) to make mini pancakes (2 inches wide).
5. Cook for 2–3 minutes per side until soft and lightly golden. Cool, cut into small pieces if needed, and serve as finger food.

Nutritional Benefits: Oats provide fiber and carbohydrates for energy and digestion; apples offer vitamin C and fiber for immunity. Ghee (if used) adds healthy fats.

5.4.2. Mini Idli

Ingredients

- 2 tbsp idli rice (or parboiled rice, rinsed)
- 1 tbsp urad dal (split black gram, rinsed)
- ¼ cup boiled water (for batter consistency)
- 1 tsp ghee (optional, for greasing or flavour)

Instructions:

1. Rinse idli rice and urad dal thoroughly, then soak separately in water for 4–6 hours.
2. Drain and blend rice with 1–2 tbsp water and urad dal with 1 tbsp water in a mixer grinder to form smooth, thick pastes. Combine both pastes, mix well, and let the batter ferment in a warm place for 8–10 hours (or overnight) until slightly bubbly.
3. Stir the fermented batter gently, adding 1–2 tbsp boiled water if needed to achieve a thick but pourable consistency.
4. Lightly grease a mini idli mold with ghee (if using). Pour small amounts of batter (about 1 tsp each) into the mini idli molds (1–2 inches wide).
5. Steam in an idli steamer or pressure cooker (without whistle) for 8–10 minutes until soft and cooked through (test with a toothpick; it should come out clean).
6. Cool to a safe temperature, remove from molds, and serve as finger food. For younger babies (10 months), mash slightly if needed.

Tip: Ensure idlis are soft and small (mini molds are ideal) to prevent choking. Test rice and urad dal separately for allergies before combining. Serve plain or with a side of mashed carrot puree to encourage self-feeding.

Tip: For variety, you can make carrot idli, spinach idli, ragi idli, moong daal idli, etc.

Nutritional Benefits: Idli rice provides digestible carbohydrates for energy; urad dal offers protein and B vitamins for growth and metabolism. Ghee (if used) adds healthy fats for brain development.

5.4.3. Ragi - Carrot Roti

Ingredients:

- 2 tbsp ragi (finger millet) flour
- ¼ cup carrot (peeled, grated, and steamed)
- 2–3 tbsp boiled water (for dough)
- 1 tsp ghee (optional, for cooking)

Instructions:

> **Tip:** Ensure pieces are soft and small to prevent choking. Ideal for self-feeding to develop pincer grasp.

1. Steam grated carrot for 5–7 minutes until soft, then mash lightly.
2. Mix ragi flour with mashed carrot and boiled water to form a soft, pliable dough.
3. Roll into small, thin rotis (2–3 inches wide) or shape into small balls and flatten slightly.
4. Cook in a pan with a touch of ghee (if using) on low heat for 1–2 minutes per side until soft but firm.
5. Cool to a safe temperature, cut into bite-sized pieces (½-inch squares), and serve as finger food.

Nutritional Benefits: Ragi provides calcium and iron for bone and blood health; carrots offer vitamin A and fiber for immunity and digestion. Ghee (if used) adds healthy fats for brain development.

5.4.4. Makhana - Sweet Potato Bites

Ingredients:

- 2 tbsp makhana (fox nuts, roasted and ground)
- ¼ cup sweet potato (peeled, cubed, steamed)
- 1 tbsp rolled oats (ground into flour)
- 2–3 tbsp boiled water (for binding)
- 1 tsp ghee (optional)

Instructions:

> **Tip:** Ensure bites are soft for safe and easy chewing.

1. Dry roast makhana on low heat for 3–4 minutes until crisp, then grind into a fine powder using a mixer grinder.
2. Steam sweet potato for 10–12 minutes until soft, then mash thoroughly.
3. Mix makhana powder, mashed sweet potato, oat flour, and water to form a soft dough.
4. Shape into small, flat bites (1–2 inches wide). Steam for 5–7 minutes until firm but soft.
5. Optionally, lightly pan-fry with ghee on low heat for 1–2 minutes per side to enhance flavour, keeping them soft.
6. Cool to a safe temperature, cut into smaller pieces if needed, and serve as finger food.

Nutritional Benefits: Makhana provides protein and magnesium for growth; sweet potato offers vitamin A and fiber for immunity and digestion; oats add fiber for energy.

5.4.5. Moong Dal - Veggie Bites

Ingredients:

- 2 tbsp moong dal (split yellow lentils, rinsed)
- ¼ cup carrot (peeled, finely chopped)
- 1 tbsp mashed sweet potato
- 1 tsp ghee (optional)

Instructions:

> **Tip:** Add a pinch of cumin powder for flavour after.

1. Rinse moong dal thoroughly, soak for 1–2 hours, then pressure cook with ½ cup water for 1-2 whistles until very soft. Mash well.
2. Steam carrots for 5–7 minutes until soft, then mash finely.
3. Mix mashed moong dal, carrot, and sweet potato to form a soft dough.
4. Shape into small, flat bites (1-inch diameter). Lightly pan-fry with ghee (if using) on low heat for 1–2 minutes per side, keeping them soft.
5. Cool to a safe temperature, cut into smaller pieces if needed, and serve as finger food.

Nutritional Benefits: Moong dal provides protein and iron for growth; carrot and sweet potato offer vitamin A and fiber for immunity and digestion.

5.4.6. Little Millet Khichdi

Ingredients:

- 1 tbsp little millet (samai, rinsed)
- 1 tbsp moong dal (split yellow lentils, rinsed)
- ¼ cup mixed vegetables (carrot and beans, finely chopped)
- ¾ cup water (for cooking)
- 1 tsp ghee (optional)

Instructions:

1. Rinse little millet and moong dal, soak for 1–2 hours, then drain.
2. Steam carrots and beans for 5–7 minutes until soft, then mash lightly.
3. Cook millet and dal with ¾ cup water in a small pan or pressure cooker (2-3 whistles) until soft and mushy.
4. Mix in mashed vegetables and ghee (if using), then cool slightly. Cool to a safe temperature and serve as finger food.

Tip: Shape Little Millet Khichdi into small, soft balls (1-inch diameter) for easy grasping to encourage self-feeding.

Nutritional Benefits: Little millet provides fiber and B vitamins for energy; moong dal offers protein and iron for growth; vegetables add vitamins A and C for immunity.

5.4.7. Sweet Potato - Carrot Mini Balls

Ingredients:

- ¼ cup sweet potato (peeled, cubed)
- ¼ cup carrot (peeled, finely chopped)
- 1 tbsp rolled oats (ground into flour)
- 1 tsp ghee (optional)
- 1–2 tbsp boiled water (for binding)

Instructions:

1. Steam sweet potato and carrot together for 10–12 minutes until very soft.
2. Mash the steamed vegetables thoroughly with a fork or blend briefly for a smooth paste.
3. Grind rolled oats into a fine powder using a mixer grinder.
4. In a bowl, mix mashed sweet potato, carrot, oat flour, and boiled water to form a soft, pliable dough. Add ghee (if using) for richness and mix well.
5. Shape into small, soft balls (1-inch diameter, about 1 tsp each). Optionally, lightly pan-fry with a touch of ghee on low heat for 1–2 minutes per side to firm up slightly, keeping them soft.
6. Cool to a safe temperature, cut into smaller pieces if needed, and serve as finger food.

Tip: Ensure balls are soft and small to prevent choking. Serve whole to encourage self-feeding.

Nutritional Benefits: Sweet potato and carrot provide vitamin A and fiber for immunity and digestion; oats add complex carbohydrates and fiber for sustained energy. Ghee (if used) contributes healthy fats for brain development.

5.4.8. Sweet Potato Sticks

Ingredients:

- 1 small sweet potato (about 100g, peeled)
- 1 tsp ghee (optional)
- 1–2 tbsp boiled water (optional, for softening)

Instructions:

1. Wash and peel the sweet potato, then cut it into thin, finger-sized sticks (about 2–3 inches long and ½-inch thick) to ensure they are easy for babies to hold.
2. Steam the sweet potato sticks for 10–12 minutes until very soft but still holding shape (test with a fork; they should be tender but not mushy).
3. Optionally, lightly coat the pan with ghee and pan-fry the steamed sticks on low heat for 1–2 minutes per side to add a slight crispness while keeping them soft inside.
4. Cool to a safe temperature. Serve as finger food.

> **Tip:** Ensure fries are soft and not crispy to prevent choking. Offer as finger food to encourage pincer grasp and self-feeding.

Nutritional Benefits: Sweet potatoes are rich in vitamin A (beta-carotene) for eye health and immunity, fiber for digestion, and carbohydrates for energy. Ghee (if used) adds healthy fats for brain development.

5.4.9. Sweet Potato - Peas Sticks

Ingredients:

- ¼ cup sweet potato (peeled, cubed)
- ¼ cup peas (fresh)
- 1 tbsp rolled oats (ground into flour)
- 1 tsp ghee (optional)

Instructions:

> **Tip:** Cut sticks into smaller pieces for easier handling.

1. Steam sweet potato and peas together for 8–10 minutes until soft, then mash thoroughly.
2. Grind rolled oats into a fine powder using a mixer grinder.
3. Mix mashed sweet potato, peas, and oat flour to form a soft dough.
4. Shape into small sticks (2 inches long, ½-inch thick). Steam for 5–7 minutes until firm but soft.
5. Optionally, lightly pan-fry with ghee on low heat for 1–2 minutes per side. Cool and serve as finger food.

Nutritional Benefits: Sweet potato and peas provide vitamin A, fiber, and antioxidants for immunity and digestion; oats add fiber for energy. Ghee (if used) supports brain development.

5.4.10. Barnyard Millet - Carrot Sticks

Ingredients:

- 2 tbsp barnyard millet (sanwa, rinsed)
- ¼ cup carrot (peeled, grated, steamed)
- 2-3 tbsp boiled water (for binding)
- ½ cup water (for cooking)
- 1 tsp ghee (optional)

> **Tip:** Cut sticks into smaller pieces for easier handling.

Instructions:

1. Rinse barnyard millet, soak for 1-2 hours, then cook with ½ cup water for 10-12 minutes until soft. Mash lightly.
2. Steam grated carrot for 5-7 minutes until soft, then mash lightly.
3. Mix cooked millet, mashed carrot, and boiled water to form a soft dough.
4. Shape into small sticks (2 inches long, ½-inch thick). Steam for 5-7 minutes until firm but soft.
5. Optionally, lightly pan-fry with ghee on low heat for 1-2 minutes per side. Cool and serve as finger food.

Nutritional Benefits: Barnyard millet provides fiber and B vitamins for energy; carrots offer vitamin A for immunity and eye health.

5.4.11. Moong Dal - Apple Sticks

Ingredients:

- 2 tbsp moong dal (split yellow lentils, rinsed)
- ¼ cup apple (peeled, grated, steamed)
- 1 tbsp rolled oats (ground into flour)
- 1 tsp ghee (optional)

> 💡 **Tip:** Serve whole to encourage chewing skills.

Instructions:

1. Rinse moong dal, soak for 1–2 hours, then pressure cook with ½ cup water for 2-3 whistles until soft. Mash thoroughly.
2. Steam the grated apple for 5–7 minutes until soft, then mash lightly.
3. Grind rolled oats into a fine powder.
4. Mix mashed moong dal, apple, oat flour, and boiled water as needed to form a soft dough. Shape into small sticks (2 inches long, ½-inch thick).
5. Steam for 5–7 minutes until firm but soft. Optionally, lightly pan-fry with ghee on low heat for 1–2 minutes per side. Cool and serve.

Nutritional Benefits: Moong dal provides protein and iron for growth; apples offer vitamin C and fiber for immunity; oats add fiber for energy.

5.4.12. Ragi - Banana Sticks

Ingredients:

- 2 tbsp ragi (finger millet) flour
- ½ ripe banana (yellow, no black spots)
- 2–3 tbsp boiled water (for binding)
- 1 tsp ghee (optional)

> **Tip:** Ensure sticks are soft and serve whole to encourage self-feeding.

Instructions:

1. Mix ragi flour with 2 tbsp water to form a smooth paste, avoiding lumps.
2. Peel and mash the banana thoroughly until smooth.
3. Combine ragi paste, mashed banana, and boiled water to form a soft, pliable dough.
4. Shape into small, finger-sized sticks (2 inches long, ½-inch thick). Steam the sticks for 8–10 minutes until firm but soft.
5. Optionally, lightly pan-fry with ghee on low heat for 1–2 minutes per side to enhance flavour, keeping them soft.
6. Cool to a safe temperature, cut into smaller pieces if needed, and serve as finger food.

Nutritional Benefits: Ragi provides calcium and iron for bone and blood health; banana offers potassium and carbohydrates for energy and digestion. Ghee (if used) adds healthy fats.

5.4.13. Foxtail Millet - Pumpkin Sticks

Ingredients:

- 2 tbsp foxtail millet (rinsed)
- ¼ cup pumpkin (peeled, cubed)
- 2–3 tbsp boiled water (for binding)
- 1 tsp ghee (optional)

Tip: Ensure sticks are soft to prevent choking.

Instructions:

1. Rinse foxtail millet, soak for 1–2 hours, then drain water.
2. Steam pumpkin cubes for 8–10 minutes until very soft, then mash finely.
3. Cook millet with ½ cup water in a small pan on low heat for 10–12 minutes until soft. Mash lightly.
4. Mix mashed pumpkin, cooked millet, and boiled water to form a soft dough. Shape into small sticks (2 inches long, ½-inch thick).
5. Steam sticks for 5–7 minutes until firm but soft. Optionally, lightly pan-fry with ghee on low heat for 1–2 minutes per side.
6. Cool to a safe temperature and serve as finger food.

Nutritional Benefits: Foxtail millet provides fiber and B vitamins for energy; pumpkin offers vitamin A and antioxidants for immunity. Ghee (if used) adds healthy fats.

5.4.14. Jowar - Banana Cakes

Ingredients:

- 2 tbsp jowar (sorghum) flour
- ½ ripe banana (yellow, no black spots)
- 2-3 tbsp boiled water (for binding)
- 1 tsp ghee (optional)

Instructions:

Tip: Ensure cakes are soft and small for easy grasping.

1. Peel and mash the banana thoroughly until smooth.
2. Mix jowar flour with mashed banana and boiled water to form a soft, pliable dough.
3. Shape into small, flat cakes (1-2 inches wide). Steam for 8-10 minutes until firm but soft.
4. Optionally, lightly pan-fry with ghee on low heat for 1-2 minutes per side to enhance flavour, keeping them soft.
5. Cool to a safe temperature and serve as finger food.

Nutritional Benefits: Jowar provides iron and fiber for blood health and digestion; banana offers potassium and carbohydrates for energy. Ghee (if used) adds healthy fats.

5.4.15. Chickpea - Pumpkin Tikki

Ingredients:

- 2 tbsp boiled chickpeas (chana, mashed)
- ¼ cup pumpkin (peeled, cubed, steamed)
- 1 tbsp rolled oats (ground into flour)
- 1 tsp ghee (optional)

> **Tip:** Ensure chickpeas are soft to avoid choking. Test each ingredient separately for allergies.

Instructions:

1. Boil chickpeas until very soft (pressure cook for 4–5 whistles), then mash thoroughly.
2. Steam pumpkin for 8–10 minutes until soft, then mash finely.
3. Grind rolled oats into a fine powder.
4. Mix mashed chickpeas, pumpkin, and oat flour to form a soft dough. Shape into small, flat tikkis (1–2 inches wide).
5. Lightly pan-fry with ghee on low heat for 1–2 minutes per side, keeping them soft. Cool and serve as finger food.

Nutritional Benefits: Chickpeas provide protein and iron for growth; pumpkin offers vitamin A and antioxidants for immunity; oats add fiber for digestion.

5.4.16. Chickpea - Sweet Potato Tikki

Ingredients:

- 2 tbsp boiled chickpeas (chana, mashed)
- ¼ cup sweet potato (peeled, cubed)
- 1 tbsp rolled oats (ground into flour)
- 1 tsp ghee (optional)

> 💡 **Tip:** Ensure chickpeas are well-cooked and soft to avoid choking.

Instructions:

1. Boil chickpeas until very soft (pressure cook for 4–5 whistles), then mash thoroughly.
2. Steam sweet potato for 10–12 minutes until soft, then mash finely.
3. Grind rolled oats into a fine powder using a mixer grinder.
4. Mix mashed chickpeas, sweet potato, and oat flour to form a soft dough.
5. Shape into small, flat tikki (1–2 inches wide). Lightly pan-fry with ghee (if using) on low heat for 1–2 minutes per side, keeping them soft.
6. Cool to a safe temperature, cut into smaller pieces if needed, and serve as finger food.

Nutritional Benefits: Chickpeas provide protein and iron for growth; sweet potato offers vitamin A and fiber for immunity and digestion; oats add fiber for energy.

5.4.17. Moong Dal - Spinach Tikki

Ingredients:

- 2 tbsp moong dal (split yellow lentils, rinsed)
- ¼ cup spinach (finely chopped, washed thoroughly)
- 1 tbsp mashed sweet potato (for binding)
- 1 tsp ghee (optional)

Instructions:

> **Tip:** Ensure spinach is well-cooked and finely mashed to avoid choking.

1. Rinse moong dal, soak for 1–2 hours, then pressure cook with ½ cup water for 2 whistles until very soft. Mash thoroughly.
2. Steam spinach for 3–4 minutes until wilted, then mash or blend finely.
3. Steam sweet potato for 10–12 minutes, then mash thoroughly.
4. Mix mashed moong dal, spinach, and sweet potato to form a soft dough. Shape into small, flat tikkis (1–2 inches wide).
5. Lightly pan-fry with ghee (if using) on low heat for 1–2 minutes per side, keeping them soft. Cool and serve as finger food.

Nutritional Benefits: Moong dal provides protein and iron for growth; spinach offers iron and vitamins A and C for immunity; sweet potato adds fiber and vitamin A.

5.4.18. Amaranth – Banana Tikki

5.4.18. Ingredients:

- 2 tbsp amaranth flour
- ½ ripe banana (yellow, no black spots)
- 2–3 tbsp boiled water (for binding)
- 1 tsp ghee (optional)

Tip: Serve whole to encourage pincer grasp development.

Instructions:

1. Mash banana thoroughly until smooth.
2. Mix amaranth flour with mashed banana and boiled water to form a soft, pliable dough.
3. Shape into small, flat tikkis (1–2 inches wide). Steam for 8–10 minutes until firm but soft.
4. Optionally, lightly pan-fry with ghee on low heat for 1–2 minutes per side, keeping them soft.
5. Cool to a safe temperature and serve as finger food.

Nutritional Benefits: Amaranth provides protein, calcium, and iron for growth and bone health; banana offers potassium and carbohydrates for energy and digestion.

5.4.19. Spinach – Jowar Tikki

Ingredients:

- 2 tbsp jowar (sorghum) flour
- ¼ cup spinach (finely chopped, washed thoroughly, steamed)
- 1 tbsp mashed sweet potato (for binding)
- 1 tsp ghee (optional)

Instructions:

Tip: Ensure spinach is well-cooked and mashed to avoid choking. Test each ingredient separately for allergies.

1. Steam spinach for 3–4 minutes until wilted, then mash or blend finely.
2. Steam sweet potato for 10–12 minutes, then mash thoroughly.
3. Mix jowar flour, mashed spinach, and sweet potato to form a soft dough.
4. Shape into small, flat tikkis (1–2 inches wide). Steam for 8–10 minutes until firm but soft.
5. Optionally, lightly pan-fry with ghee on low heat for 1–2 minutes per side. Cool and serve as finger food.

Nutritional Benefits: Jowar provides iron and fiber for blood health and digestion; spinach offers vitamins A and C for immunity; sweet potato adds vitamin A and fiber.

5.4.20. Mix Veg Rice

Ingredients:

- 2 tbsp rice (preferably brown or parboiled, rinsed)
- ¼ cup mixed vegetables (carrot, peas, and french beans, finely chopped)
- ¾ cup water (for cooking)
- 1 tsp ghee (optional)

Instructions:

> **Tip:** Serve slightly textured to encourage chewing, or as soft finger food in small portions.

1. Rinse rice thoroughly, soak for 1-2 hours, then drain water.
2. Steam mixed vegetables (carrot, peas, French beans) for 5–7 minutes until soft, then mash or blend finely.
3. Cook rice with ¾ cup water in a small pan or pressure cooker (1-2 whistles) for 8–10 minutes until soft and mushy.
4. Mix in mashed vegetables and ghee (if using), stirring well to combine.
5. Blend for a smooth texture or keep slightly chunky. Cool and serve warm.

Nutritional Benefits: Rice provides digestible carbohydrates for energy; mixed vegetables offer vitamin A, fiber, and antioxidants for immunity and digestion. Ghee (if used) supports brain development.

5.5. Portion Sizes

Mess is Okay !! Allow exploration, as messy eating supports sensory development and independence.

At 10–12 months, a balanced meal becomes crucial, which includes proteins, carbohydrates, fats, and vital nutrients, including breast milk or formula. Feeding schedules should align with hunger cues and fullness signals.

- Offer 1/4–1/2 cup (60–120 ml) per meal and 1–2 tbsp per snack, adjusting based on hunger cues.
- Rotate proteins, vegetables, and fruits daily to ensure nutrient diversity and flavour exposure.
- Let your baby guide intake; avoid force-feeding to prevent aversions.

Tip: Offer 1–2 tsp water in a lidless cup during meals to practice sipping, avoiding sugary drinks like fruit juices.

6: Special Considerations and Tips

As your baby grows from 6 to 12 months, their food journey becomes a delightful blend of exploration and discovery. In Indian homes, where meals are a vibrant expression of love and culture, parents face unique challenges, such as picky eating, food refusal, dietary restrictions, and busy schedules. This chapter offers practical strategies to address these hurdles, featuring meal prep hacks for on-the-go feeding.

6.1. Addressing Picky Eating and Food Refusals

Picky eating and food refusals are common between 6 and 12 months as babies assert their independence and explore their sensory preferences. This period coincides with significant physical, cognitive, and emotional changes, which contribute to selective eating behaviors. Understanding the science behind these behaviors helps parents respond with patience and creativity.

6.1.1. Why Does Picky Eating Happen?

Picky eating, typically normal and temporary, in babies 6-12 months, often appears during weaning to solids, caused by developmental and sensory factors. Key reasons include:

- **Sensory Overload and Neophobia:** Babies encounter new tastes, textures, and smells, triggering an innate wariness of unfamiliar foods to avoid potential toxins. Bitter or strong flavours (e.g., vegetables) are often rejected due to sensitive taste buds.
- **Oral Motor Challenges:** Developing skills for chewing and swallowing make chunky or hard foods difficult, leading to refusals unrelated to taste.
- **Emerging Independence:** Babies assert control by rejecting spoon-feeding or unfamiliar items, signaling growing autonomy around 9 months.
- **Appetite Fluctuations:** Growth slows after 6 months, reducing hunger; teething pain further discourages eating.
- **Early Feeding Practices:** Late or limited solids introduction, or parental pressure, can foster selectivity

6.1.2. Strategies to Overcome Picky Eating

- **Offer Variety Repeatedly**: It may take 15–20 exposures for a baby to accept a new food. Serve small amounts of rejected foods (e.g., spinach puree) alongside favorites without pressure.
- **Model Eating**: Eat with your baby at the family table to demonstrate enjoyment of diverse foods. Social modeling boosts acceptance. Engage grandparents or siblings in feeding to create a positive and social mealtime environment.
- **Engage Senses**: Present colorful foods (e.g., orange carrots, green peas) and vary textures (smooth purees to soft finger foods) to stimulate curiosity.
- **Respect Hunger Cues**: Avoid force-feeding, as it can lead to aversions. Let your baby guide intake, offering 1–2 tbsp initially and increasing as they show interest.
- **Indian Context**: Introduce familiar flavours like mild cumin in khichdi to make new foods feel comforting. Use seasonal produce (e.g., mangoes in summer) to keep meals exciting.

6.1.3. Handling Food Refusals

- **Stay Calm**: Refusals are not personal. Respond with patience to avoid creating negative associations with food.
- **Adjust Timing**: Offer meals when your baby is hungry but not overly tired, aligning with family routines (e.g., mid-morning or early evening).
- **Check for Discomfort**: Teething or illness may cause refusals. Offer softer foods (e.g., mashed banana) during teething phases.
- **Consult a Paediatrician**: Persistent refusals or weight concerns may signal underlying issues. Seek advice from your paediatrician.

6.2. Meal Prep Hacks for Busy Parents and On-the-Go Feeding

Busy schedules and travel are common in Indian families, but meal prep hacks ensure your baby enjoys nutritious, homemade foods anytime, anywhere.

6.2.1. Meal Prep Strategies

- **One-Pot Meals**: Cook khichdi or vegetable-dal blends in a pressure cooker for quick, nutrient-dense meals. Adjust textures accordingly.
- **Repurpose Family Foods**: Modify family dishes (e.g., unsalted dal, mashed roti) for babies, saving time.
- **Storage Labeling**: Use airtight containers or ziplock bags, labeling with dates (only dry ready-to-eat foods like e.g., "Cerelac Powder 25/06/2025") to track freshness. Storing cooked meals is not advisable, as the meal may undergo taste alteration, leading to a negative association with the meal subsequently.

6.2.2. On-the-Go Feeding Tips

- **Portable Containers**: Use BPA-free, leak-proof containers to carry purees or finger foods like mini idlis.
- **Finger Food Kits**: Pack soft, non-messy foods (e.g., banana slices) in small dabbas (stainless steel) for travel or outings to parks or temples.
- **Thermal Bags**: Keep foods at safe temperatures using insulated lunch bags, ideal for long car rides or train journeys.
- **Hygiene on the Go**: Carry sanitized spoons, bibs, and water-based hand wipes to maintain cleanliness at restaurants or relatives' homes.

7: FAQs and Troubleshooting

FAQs and Troubleshooting for Parents

Feeding your baby between 6 and 12 months is an exciting journey, but it can come with questions and challenges. As parents, you may worry about whether your baby is eating enough, reacting to new foods, or transitioning to solids smoothly. This chapter addresses common concerns and guides you on when to seek professional assistance.

7.1. Common Feeding Concerns

7.1.1. Gagging vs. Choking: What's the Difference?

Concern: Many parents panic when their baby gags or coughs while eating, fearing it's choking.

- **Gagging** is a normal reflex as babies learn to chew and swallow new textures. It happens when food triggers the gag reflex at the back of the mouth, helping babies move food safely. For example, your baby might gag on a lumpy vegetable khichdi but spit it out naturally. Gagging is a protective mechanism controlled by the brainstem.
- **Choking** is a serious blockage of the airway, often caused by large or hard foods. Signs include inability to cry, cough, or breathe, requiring immediate action. Choking risks increase with foods like whole nuts, raw veggies, or grapes, which are unsafe until age 4.
- **Emergency Action**: If choking occurs (silent with blue lips), perform infant choking first aid (back blows and chest thrusts). Keep a choking rescue device at home, and you can also call emergency services (108 in India) or the nearest medical facility and seek immediate first aid.

Tip: Always supervise your baby during meals and ensure they sit upright in a highchair or on your lap.

7.1.2. Slow Weight Gain: Is My Baby Growing Enough?

Concern: Parents often worry if their baby isn't gaining weight as expected, especially when transitioning to solids.

Babies grow rapidly in the first year, but growth rates vary. Slow weight gain may result from inadequate food intake, frequent illnesses, or normal variations. Breast milk or formula remains the primary nutritional source until 12 months, with solids complementing it.

Tips:

- Continue breastfeeding or formula to ensure adequate intake.
- Offer iron-rich foods like masoor dal, ragi porridge, starting with 1–2 teaspoons and increasing to 3 meals by 12 months.
- Include energy-dense foods like ghee (in moderation) or mashed avocado to boost energy intake.
- Track growth monthly. If weight gain is consistently low, consult a doctor.

7.1.3. Food Allergies: How Do I Spot and Prevent Them?

Concern: Parents worry about allergic reactions when introducing new foods like nuts.

Food allergies occur when the immune system reacts to certain proteins, causing symptoms like rashes, vomiting, or breathing difficulties. Common allergens include peanuts and dairy, but early introduction (after 6 months) may reduce allergy risk.

Tips:

- Introduce one new food every 2–3 days to monitor reactions. Start with a small amount (e.g., 1/4 teaspoon).
- Watch for signs of allergies: rashes, hives, vomiting, diarrhea, or breathing problems. Stop the food and consult a pediatrician if symptoms appear.
- Call emergency services (108 in India) or the nearest medical facility if your baby struggles to breathe or shows severe swelling.
- Common Indian allergens include curd, paneer, and ground nuts. Offer these in pureed form initially, ensuring no added salt or sugar.
- If there's a family history of allergies, consult a doctor before introducing high-risk foods.

7.1.4. Transitioning to Solids: Why Is My Baby Struggling?

Concern: Some babies resist solids or prefer breast milk/formula.

Transitioning to solids requires coordination of swallowing and chewing, which develops gradually. Resistance may stem from unfamiliar textures, teething discomfort, or fullness from milk. Premature introduction or rapid texture changes can cause resistance.

Tips:

- Ensure your baby shows readiness signs: sitting with minimal support, opening mouth for food, and turning away when full.
- Offer solids when your baby is hungry, before breast milk or formula, to encourage acceptance.
- For premature babies, consult a pediatrician, as they may need solids delayed by 1-2 months.

When to Consult a Healthcare Professional

Seek help from the nearest medical facility or pediatrician if you notice:

- **Persistent Slow Weight Gain**
- **Severe Allergic Reactions:**
- **Choking Incidents**
- **Refusal to Eat Solids**
- **Unusual Symptoms** (Frequent diarrhea/vomiting, blood in stool, or excessive fussiness during meals may signal allergies, intolerances, or infections.)

8: Homemade Porridge – Premixes and Coconut Milk

Rice - Sabudana Porridge - Premix

Ingredients:

- 2 tbsp rice (preferably brown or parboiled, rinsed)
- 1 tbsp sabudana (sago/tapioca pearls, rinsed)
- 1 tbsp urad dal (split black gram, rinsed)
- 4 cashews (optional, for 8+ months)
- 1 cup water (for cooking)
- 1–2 tbsp breast milk or formula (optional, for thinning)

Instructions:

1. Wash the rice, sabudana, and urad dal thoroughly, then soak for 2–3 hours. Drain the water and air-dry on a clean cloth.
2. Dry roast cashews (if using) on low heat for 2–3 minutes until lightly fragrant, then cool.
3. Dry roast rice, sabudana, and urad dal separately on low heat for 3–4 minutes until slightly golden. Cool completely.
4. Grind roasted rice, sabudana, urad dal, and cashews into a fine powder using a mixer grinder. Sieve to ensure smoothness.
5. To prepare, mix 1–2 tbsp of the porridge-premix with 1 cup of water in a pan. Cook on low heat for 5–7 minutes, stirring to avoid lumps, until it forms a smooth porridge. Add breast milk or formula for flavour, if desired. Cool to a safe temperature and serve.

Tip: Sabudana is gentle on the stomach, perfect for 6+ months. Serve in small portions initially to ensure the baby tolerates the mix.

Nutritional Benefits: Sabudana and rice provide easily digestible carbohydrates for quick energy; urad dal adds protein and B vitamins for growth and metabolism. Cashews (if used) contribute healthy fats for brain development.

Storage: Keep the dry porridge-premix powder in an airtight container in a cool, dry place for up to 1 month.

Barley - Moong Dal Porridge - Premix

Ingredients:

- 2 tbsp barley (pearl barley, rinsed)
- 1 tbsp moong dal (split yellow lentils, rinsed)
- 1 tbsp rice (preferably brown or parboiled, rinsed)
- 4 walnuts (optional, for 8+ months)
- 1 cup water (for cooking)
- 1–2 tbsp breast milk or formula (optional, for thinning and flavour)

Instructions:

1. Wash the barley, moong dal, and rice thoroughly, then soak for 2–3 hours. Drain water and air-dry on a clean cloth.
2. Dry roast walnuts (if using) on low heat for 2–3 minutes until lightly fragrant, then cool.

> **Tip:** Barley is soothing for the stomach, ideal for 7+ months. Test each ingredient separately for allergies before combining, especially walnuts.

3. Dry roast barley, moong dal, and rice separately on low heat for 3–4 minutes until slightly golden. Cool completely.
4. Grind roasted barley, moong dal, rice, and walnuts into a fine powder using a mixer grinder. Sieve to ensure a smooth texture.
5. To prepare, mix 1–2 tbsp of the porridge-premix powder with 1 cup of water in a pan. Cook on low heat for 5–7 minutes, stirring continuously to avoid lumps, until it forms a smooth porridge. Add breast milk or formula for creaminess, if desired. Cool to a safe temperature and serve.

Nutritional Benefits: Barley provides fiber and B vitamins for digestion and energy; moong dal adds protein and iron for growth; rice offers digestible carbohydrates. Walnuts (if used) contribute omega-3 fatty acids for brain development.

Storage: Store the dry porridge-premix powder in an airtight container in a cool, dry place for up to 1 month.

Jowar - Lentil Porridge Premix

Ingredients:

- 2 tbsp jowar (sorghum) flour
- 1 tbsp chana dal (split chickpeas, rinsed)
- 1 tbsp rice (preferably brown or parboiled, rinsed)
- 5 almonds (skin removed, optional, 8+ months)
- 1 cup water (for cooking)
- 1–2 tbsp breast milk or formula (optional, for thinning)

Instructions:

1. Wash chana dal and rice thoroughly, soak for 2–3 hours, then drain and air-dry completely.
2. Dry roast almonds (if using) on low heat for 2–3 minutes until fragrant, then cool.
3. Dry roast chana dal and rice separately on low heat for 3–4 minutes until lightly golden. Cool completely.
4. Grind jowar flour, roasted chana dal, rice, and almonds into a fine powder using a mixer grinder. Sieve for a smooth texture.
5. To prepare, mix 1–2 tbsp of the porridge-premix powder with 1 cup of water in a pan. Cook on low heat for 5–7 minutes, stirring to prevent lumps, until it forms a smooth porridge. Add breast milk or formula for a creamier texture. Cool and serve.

Tip: Jowar is gluten-free and ideal for 7+ months. For 8+ months, mix with a small amount of mashed apple for sweetness, after checking for allergies.

Nutritional Benefits: Jowar is rich in iron, fiber, and antioxidants for blood health and digestion; chana dal provides protein for growth; rice adds energy. Almonds (if used) offer healthy fats and vitamin E for brain and skin health.

Storage: Store the porridge-premix powder in an airtight container in a cool, dry place for up to 1 month.

Ragi + Moong Dal Porridge – Premix

Ingredients:

- 2 tbsp ragi (finger millet) flour
- 1 tbsp moong dal (split yellow lentils, rinsed)
- 1 tbsp rice (preferably brown or parboiled, rinsed)
- 5 cashews (optional, for 8+ months)
- 1 cup water (for cooking)
- 1–2 tbsp breast milk or formula (optional, for thinning and flavour)

> **Tip:** Start with a small serving (½ tsp powder) for 6–7 months to check digestibility. For 8+ months, add a pinch of cardamom for flavour (avoid sugar or honey for babies under 1 year).

Instructions:

1. Wash the rice and moong dal thoroughly, then soak for 2–3 hours. Drain water and air-dry on a clean cloth.
2. Dry roast cashews (if using) on low heat for 2–3 minutes until lightly fragrant, then cool.
3. Dry roast rice and moong dal separately on low heat for 3–4 minutes until slightly golden. Cool completely.
4. Grind ragi flour, roasted rice, moong dal, and cashews into a fine powder using a mixer grinder. Sieve to remove coarse particles.
5. To prepare, mix 1–2 tbsp of the porridge-premix powder with 1 cup of water in a pan. Cook on low heat for 5–7 minutes, stirring to avoid lumps, until it forms a smooth porridge. Add breast milk or formula for creaminess, if desired. Cool to a safe temperature and serve.

Nutritional Benefits: Ragi provides calcium and iron for bone and blood health; moong dal adds protein for growth; rice offers carbohydrates for energy. Cashews (if used) contribute healthy fats for brain development.

Storage: Store the dry porridge-premix powder in an airtight container in a cool, dry place for up to 1 month.

Oats - Lentil Porridge - Premix

Ingredients:

- 2 tbsp rolled oats
- 1 tbsp masoor dal (red lentils, rinsed)
- 1 tbsp wheat dalia (broken wheat, rinsed)
- 4 almonds (skin removed, optional, 8+ months)
- 1 cup water (for cooking)
- 1–2 tbsp breast milk or formula (optional, for thinning)

Instructions:

1. Wash masoor dal and wheat dalia thoroughly, soak for 2 hours, then drain and air-dry completely.
2. Dry roast almonds (if using) on low heat for 2–3 minutes until fragrant, then cool.
3. Dry roast oats, masoor dal, and wheat dalia separately on low heat for 3–4 minutes until slightly golden. Cool completely.
4. Grind roasted oats, dal, dalia, and almonds into a fine powder using a mixer grinder. Sieve for a smooth texture.
5. To prepare, mix 1–2 tbsp of the porridge-premix powder with 1 cup of water in a pan. Cook on low heat for 5–7 minutes, stirring continuously to prevent lumps, until it forms a smooth porridge. Add breast milk or formula for a creamier texture. Cool and serve.

Tip: Introduce oats and wheat gradually to ensure the baby tolerates grains. For 8+ months, mix with mashed banana for natural sweetness.

Nutritional Benefits: Oats and wheat dalia provide fiber for digestion and sustained energy; masoor dal adds protein and iron for growth and blood health. Almonds (if used) offer healthy fats for brain development.

Storage: Store the porridge-premix powder in an airtight container in a cool, dry place for up to 1 month.

Multi-Grain Porridge - Premix

Ingredients:

- 1 tbsp ragi (finger millet) flour
- 1 tbsp rice (brown or parboiled, rinsed)
- 1 tbsp moong dal (split yellow lentils, rinsed)
- 1 tbsp sabudana (sago/tapioca pearls)
- 5 pistachios (optional, for 8+ months)
- 1 cup water (for cooking)
- 1–2 tbsp breast milk or formula (optional, for thinning)

Instructions:

1. Wash the rice, moong dal, and sabudana thoroughly, then soak for 2–3 hours. Drain water and air-dry on a clean cloth.
2. Dry roast pistachios (if using) on low heat for 2–3 minutes until fragrant, then cool.
3. Dry roast rice, moong dal, and sabudana separately on low heat for 3–4 minutes until lightly golden. Cool completely.
4. Grind ragi flour, roasted rice, moong dal, sabudana, and pistachios into a fine powder using a mixer grinder. Sieve to ensure smoothness.
5. To prepare, mix 1–2 tbsp of the porridge-premix powder with 1 cup of water in a pan. Cook on low heat for 5–7 minutes, stirring to avoid lumps, until it forms a smooth porridge. Add breast milk or formula for flavour, if desired. Cool to a safe temperature and serve.

Tip: Sabudana is gentle on the stomach, ideal for 7+ months. Test each ingredient separately for allergies before combining in this mix.

Nutritional Benefits: Ragi and moong dal provide calcium, iron, and protein for bone and muscle growth; rice and sabudana offer easily digestible carbohydrates for energy. Pistachios (if used) add healthy fats and vitamins.

Storage: Store the dry porridge-premix powder in an airtight container in a cool, dry place for up to 1 month.

Makhana - Poha Porridge - Premix

Ingredients:

- 2 tbsp makhana (fox nuts, whole)
- 2 tbsp poha (flattened rice, thin variety, rinsed)
- 1 tbsp rolled oats
- 5 cashews
- 1 pinch cardamom powder (optional, for 8+ months)
- 1 cup water (for cooking)
- 1–2 tbsp breast milk or formula (optional, for thinning and flavour)

Instructions:

1. Rinse poha briefly to remove impurities, then drain and air-dry completely on a clean cloth.
2. Dry roast makhana on low heat for 3–4 minutes until crisp (they should break easily). Cool completely.
3. Dry roast poha on low heat for 2–3 minutes until slightly crisp but not browned. Cool completely.
4. Dry roast rolled oats on low heat for 2–3 minutes until lightly fragrant. Cool completely.
5. Dry roast cashews on low heat for 2–3 minutes until golden. Cool completely.
6. Grind roasted makhana, poha, oats, cashews, and a pinch of cardamom powder into a fine powder using a mixer grinder. Sieve to ensure a smooth texture, discarding any coarse bits.
7. To prepare, mix 1–2 tbsp of the porridge-premix powder with 1 cup of water in a pan. Cook on low heat for 5–7 minutes, stirring continuously to avoid lumps, until it forms a smooth porridge. Add breast milk or formula for a creamier texture, if desired. Cool to a safe temperature and serve.

> **Tip:** Introduce makhana and cashews separately first to check for allergies, as they are potential allergens. For 8+ months, serve in small portions (½ tsp powder initially) to ensure baby tolerates the mix.

Nutritional Benefits: Makhana provides protein and magnesium for growth and muscle health; poha and oats offer digestible carbohydrates and fiber for energy and digestion; cashews add healthy fats for brain development. Cardamom enhances flavour and aids digestion (in small amounts).

Storage: Store the dry porridge-premix powder in an airtight container in a cool, dry place for up to 1 month.

Homemade Coconut Milk

Ingredients:

- 1 cup fresh coconut (grated, from a mature coconut)
- 1–1.5 cups warm boiled water (filtered, for blending)

Instructions:

1. Crack open a fresh coconut, remove the white flesh, and grate it finely using a manual grater or food processor. Ensure the coconut is fresh (white, firm, and free of mold or odor).
2. Place the grated coconut in a mixer grinder or blender. Add 1 cup warm (not hot) boiled water to aid blending and ensure safety for babies.
3. Blend on high speed for 1–2 minutes until the mixture is smooth and creamy.
4. Strain the mixture through a clean muslin cloth or fine mesh sieve into a bowl, squeezing firmly to extract as much milk as possible. The first extract will be thick.
5. (Optional for thinner milk) Return the coconut pulp to the blender, add ½ cup warm boiled water, blend again, and strain to get a second, lighter extract. Combine with the first extract if a thinner consistency is desired for baby recipes.
6. Cool to room temperature and use immediately for maximum freshness. Serve plain (in small amounts) or use in baby recipes like kheer or porridge.

Nutritional Benefits: Coconut milk provides healthy fats (medium-chain fatty acids) for brain development and energy, along with small amounts of vitamins C and E for immunity. It's a dairy-free option for babies who tolerate it well.

Storage: Store in an airtight glass container in the fridge for up to 24 hours. Shake gently before use, as it may separate. Do not freeze, as it can alter texture and safety for babies. Discard if it develops an off smell or taste.

💡 **Tip: Introduce coconut milk in small amounts (1–2 tsp) mixed with familiar foods (e.g., Carrot Kheer from your list) to test for allergies. Use only fresh, homemade coconut milk without additives for babies. Avoid serving plain in large quantities; dilute with water or mix into recipes for 10–12 months to aid digestion.**

Age Preference: 8+ months (in small amounts, mixed with other foods; 10–12 months for regular use in recipes like kheer or porridge, after allergy testing).

A Final Note of Encouragement

Dear parents, feeding your baby is a journey of love, patience, and discovery. Embrace the mess of mashed bananas, the giggles over a new flavour, and the pride of watching your baby grow. Whether you're blending a comforting dal puree or offering a soft paratha bite, you're nurturing your baby's body and soul with the flavours of different cultures of India. Experiment with our recipes, adapt them to your family's tastes, and enjoy this special time. Your efforts today are building a healthy foundation for tomorrow.